How Artificial Intelligence Will Transform Your Business in 2024: Be the First to Know!

Index

Introduction

We live in an era of rapid change, where technology not only transforms how we work and interact but also shapes the future of business. Artificial Intelligence (AI), once a concept confined to science fiction, is now becoming an integral part of the business landscape. Its potential to revolutionize processes, strategic decisions, and customer experiences opens up new horizons of opportunity for companies.

The year 2024 promises to be a pivotal moment in this revolution. Advances in AI are already demonstrating significant impacts on business efficiency and innovation. From automating routine tasks to deep data analysis and predictive analytics—AI offers unprecedented opportunities for optimization and growth.

However, alongside these opportunities, AI brings new challenges. Issues related to data security, ethical considerations, and the need for workforce adaptation require careful analysis and strategic planning.

This book is dedicated to exploring how AI will transform businesses in 2024. We will examine key trends, the integration of AI into various business processes, and discuss how you can adapt to these changes to remain competitive in a rapidly evolving world.

Prepare to discover how AI can become a powerful ally in your journey to success and how you can leverage its capabilities to create innovative solutions and achieve your business goals.

The Evolution of Artificial Intelligence

The Rise of AI: A Comprehensive Overview

Artificial Intelligence (AI) has evolved from a nascent idea into one of the most transformative technologies of the 21st century. This chapter delves into the history, development, applications, challenges, and future of AI, providing a comprehensive overview of its rise and impact on modern society.

Historical Context and Early Developments

AI's origins trace back to the mid-20th century, with theoretical foundations laid by pioneers like Alan Turing. Turing's 1950 paper, "Computing Machinery and Intelligence," posed the question of whether machines could think and introduced the concept of the Turing Test as a measure of machine intelligence. Early AI research focused on symbolic reasoning and problem-solving, with the aim of creating machines that could emulate human cognitive functions.

The first AI programs, developed in the 1950s and 1960s, were based on symbolic logic and heuristic approaches. These early systems, such as the Logic Theorist and the General Problem Solver, demonstrated that machines could solve complex problems through programmed rules. However, progress was limited by the computational power and data availability of the time, leading to what is often referred to as the "AI Winter," a period of reduced funding and interest in AI research.

The Emergence of Machine Learning

The 1980s and 1990s marked a significant shift with the rise of machine learning (ML), a subset of AI that focuses on developing algorithms capable of learning from and making predictions based on data. This period saw the advent of new techniques such as neural networks, which attempt to mimic the human brain's structure and function. However, early neural networks faced challenges due to limited computational resources and insufficient data.

The resurgence of AI in the 2000s can be attributed to three key factors: the explosion of big data, advances in computational power, and improvements in algorithms. The availability of vast amounts of data and the development of powerful GPUs (Graphics Processing Units) enabled researchers to train more sophisticated models. Concurrently, the refinement of algorithms, including deep learning techniques, allowed machines to learn from data with unprecedented accuracy.

Breakthroughs in AI: The Deep Learning Revolution

The 2010s witnessed a renaissance in AI, driven by breakthroughs in deep learning. Deep learning, a subset of machine learning, involves training neural networks with multiple layers (hence "deep") to perform complex tasks. Landmark achievements during this period include:

Image Recognition: In 2012, a deep learning model called AlexNet won the ImageNet competition, drastically improving image classification accuracy and demonstrating the power of convolutional neural networks (CNNs).

Natural Language Processing: The development of models like Word2Vec and later, transformer-based models such as BERT and GPT-3, revolutionized natural language processing (NLP). These models enable machines to understand and generate human language with high proficiency.

Autonomous Systems: AI-powered systems, such as self-driving cars and drones, began to transition from experimental technologies to practical applications. Companies like Tesla and Waymo have pioneered advancements in autonomous vehicle technology, showcasing the potential of AI in reshaping transportation.

AI in Everyday Life

AI's integration into daily life is profound and pervasive. In consumer technology, AI algorithms power recommendation systems on platforms like Netflix and Amazon, enhancing user experience through personalized suggestions. Virtual assistants such as Siri, Google Assistant, and Alexa leverage natural language processing to interact with users and perform tasks.

In the healthcare sector, AI is transforming diagnostics and treatment. Machine learning models assist in identifying diseases from medical images, predicting patient outcomes, and personalizing treatment plans. AI-driven drug discovery is accelerating the development of new pharmaceuticals by analyzing vast datasets and simulating biological processes.

The financial industry also benefits from AI through algorithmic trading, fraud detection, and personalized financial services. AI systems analyze market trends and execute trades at high speeds, while fraud detection algorithms monitor transactions for anomalies and potential threats.

Challenges and Ethical Considerations

Despite its advancements, AI presents significant challenges and ethical concerns. Key issues include:

Data Privacy: AI systems often rely on vast amounts of personal data. Ensuring the protection of this data and maintaining user privacy is a critical concern.

Bias and Fairness: AI algorithms can perpetuate and amplify biases present in training data, leading to unfair or discriminatory outcomes. Addressing these biases requires careful design and ongoing monitoring.

Job Displacement: The automation of tasks traditionally performed by humans raises concerns about job displacement and the future of work. Strategies for workforce adaptation and reskilling are essential to mitigate these effects.

Autonomous Systems and Safety: As AI systems become more autonomous, ensuring their safety and reliability is paramount. The development of robust safety protocols and regulatory frameworks is necessary to address potential risks.

The Future of AI

The future of AI holds exciting possibilities and potential challenges. Key areas of focus include:

Quantum Computing: The development of quantum computers promises to revolutionize AI by enabling the processing of complex problems that are currently intractable for classical computers. Quantum algorithms could lead to breakthroughs in fields such as cryptography, optimization, and drug discovery.

AI and Ethics: The establishment of ethical guidelines and regulatory frameworks will be crucial in guiding the responsible development and deployment of AI technologies. Collaborations between researchers, policymakers, and industry leaders will be essential in addressing ethical concerns and ensuring AI benefits society as a whole.

General AI: The pursuit of artificial general intelligence (AGI), machines with human-like cognitive abilities, remains a long-term goal. While AGI is still speculative, its development would represent a monumental achievement with profound implications for humanity.

The rise of AI signifies a transformative era in human history. From its theoretical beginnings to its current status as a driving force behind technological innovation, AI has reshaped industries and daily life. As AI continues to evolve, navigating its development with foresight and responsibility will be crucial in harnessing its full potential while addressing its challenges. The future of AI promises to unlock new possibilities and redefine our relationship with technology, underscoring the importance of thoughtful stewardship in this dynamic field.

Why 2024 is a Pivotal Year for AI

As artificial intelligence (AI) advances at an exponential pace, 2024 stands out as a crucial year that could shape the trajectory of AI for decades to come. From groundbreaking technological innovations to regulatory shifts and ethical considerations, this year marks a critical juncture in AI's development. The convergence of powerful computational models, expanding industry adoption, and evolving societal concerns highlights 2024 as a pivotal year in AI's evolution.

Technological Milestones: Beyond Deep Learning

The past few years have been dominated by the success of deep learning models, particularly in areas such as image recognition, natural language processing, and autonomous systems. However, 2024 is witnessing the emergence of new paradigms that go beyond the current capabilities of AI.

Generative AI and Multimodal Systems: While generative AI, like OpenAI's GPT models and DALL-E, has been making headlines for its ability to create text, images, and even music, 2024 has seen these models mature into more sophisticated, multimodal systems. AI systems can now process and generate outputs across different types of media, seamlessly integrating text, images, audio, and video. This has revolutionized creative industries, communication, and entertainment by making content creation faster, more accessible, and highly personalized.

AI-Powered Innovation in Science: 2024 has also been pivotal in expanding AI's role in scientific discovery. Machine learning algorithms are being used to predict molecular structures, accelerate drug discovery, and analyze vast datasets from space exploration and climate change research. For example, AI systems have begun making contributions to solving complex problems like protein folding, which is critical to understanding diseases and developing new treatments.

Advances in Quantum AI: The integration of quantum computing with AI is another technological frontier that is gaining momentum in 2024. Quantum AI holds the potential to solve problems that are currently beyond the reach of classical AI systems. By leveraging quantum algorithms, researchers aim to tackle challenges in optimization, cryptography, and material science, paving the way for breakthroughs in industries from pharmaceuticals to logistics.

AI as an Industry Force: Widespread Adoption and Automation

In 2024, AI is no longer a niche technology confined to research labs or tech giants. It has become a core driver of innovation and growth across multiple industries.

AI in Healthcare: The healthcare sector has experienced a massive shift in 2024 due to AI's increased role in diagnostics, personalized medicine, and healthcare management. AI-driven predictive models can now analyze patient data to anticipate health outcomes, allowing for earlier interventions and customized treatment plans. Additionally, AI-powered robotic surgery and telemedicine are reshaping the way healthcare is delivered, improving accessibility and outcomes globally.

AI in Manufacturing and Automation: Industrial automation has reached new heights in 2024, with AI at its core. Advanced AI algorithms are enabling fully autonomous factories where robots handle everything from production to quality control, with minimal human intervention. This rise of AI in manufacturing is significantly reducing costs, increasing productivity, and reshaping global supply chains.

AI in Finance and Business: Financial institutions are relying heavily on AI to streamline operations, improve decision-making, and mitigate risk. AI systems now analyze vast quantities of data to optimize trading, predict market trends, and detect fraudulent activities. Additionally, AI-driven insights are empowering businesses to make more data-informed decisions, improving marketing strategies, customer engagement, and overall profitability.

Regulatory and Ethical Turning Points

While AI's technological advancements have been impressive, 2024 has also emerged as a critical year for addressing the ethical and regulatory frameworks surrounding AI. As AI systems grow more powerful and autonomous, governments, corporations, and society at large are grappling with how to regulate AI in ways that ensure safety, fairness, and accountability.

Global AI Regulation: In 2024, several major economies are implementing comprehensive regulations to govern AI development and deployment. The European Union has taken the lead with its **AI Act**, which introduces strict guidelines for AI systems deemed to carry high risks, such as those used in critical sectors like healthcare, law enforcement, and transportation. The act sets a precedent for other nations to follow, balancing innovation with consumer protection and ethical accountability.

AI and Data Privacy: With the growing use of AI in everyday applications, concerns about data privacy have reached a tipping point. In 2024, new data protection regulations have come into effect, forcing companies to rethink how they collect, store, and process personal data. This year has seen the rise of privacy-preserving AI technologies, such as **federated learning** and **differential privacy**, which allow AI models to be trained on decentralized data without compromising individual privacy.

AI Ethics and Bias Mitigation: Another pivotal focus in 2024 is addressing AI bias and ensuring ethical AI systems. Researchers and companies are increasingly prioritizing fairness, transparency, and explainability in AI models. Algorithms must now undergo rigorous testing to avoid biased outcomes, especially in sensitive areas like hiring, law enforcement, and lending. Moreover, ethical AI boards are being established within organizations to oversee the responsible development and deployment of AI technologies.

AI and the Future of Work

One of the most profound shifts in 2024 is AI's impact on the labor market. As AI-driven automation becomes more widespread, industries are experiencing significant transformations in their workforce dynamics.

Job Displacement and Workforce Reskilling: The automation of routine and manual tasks has accelerated in 2024, leading to fears of job displacement across several sectors. However, forward-thinking companies are investing heavily in workforce reskilling programs, helping employees adapt to the changing landscape. AI itself is being used to facilitate these transitions, with AI-powered training platforms offering personalized learning paths to upskill workers in fields like data science, cybersecurity, and advanced manufacturing.

The Rise of AI-Collaborative Workforces: Rather than replacing human workers entirely, AI is increasingly being used to augment human capabilities. In fields such as design, engineering, and marketing, AI systems are enabling workers to focus on creative, strategic, and high-value tasks while automating repetitive processes. This has led to the emergence of "collaborative intelligence," where humans and AI systems work together to achieve outcomes that neither could accomplish alone.

The Geopolitical AI Race

2024 is also marked by the intensifying global competition in AI, with nations vying for dominance in this critical technology. AI has become a central aspect of national security, economic power, and geopolitical influence.

AI and National Security: AI is increasingly being integrated into defense and intelligence operations, from autonomous drones to AI-driven cybersecurity systems. In 2024, nations are investing heavily in developing AI capabilities for military purposes, raising concerns about the militarization of AI and the potential for new forms of warfare. Efforts are underway to establish international agreements and norms for the responsible use of AI in defense.

China and the U.S. Leading the AI Race: The race for AI supremacy in 2024 continues to be dominated by China and the United States. Both countries have made significant investments in AI research, talent development, and industrial adoption. China's national AI strategy, coupled with its access to vast datasets, has allowed it to rapidly advance AI capabilities, while the U.S. remains a global leader in AI innovation through its technology giants and academic institutions.

2024 is proving to be a watershed year for artificial intelligence, marking a turning point in the technology's development, integration, and regulation. As AI continues to unlock new possibilities across industries, it also brings with it unprecedented challenges and opportunities. This year will likely be remembered as a time when the balance between innovation and ethics, automation and employment, and national interests and global cooperation came into sharp focus.

As we look ahead, the choices made in 2024 will have lasting implications on how AI shapes the future of humanity, emphasizing the need for thoughtful, responsible, and collaborative approaches to this transformative technology.

Enhanced Machine Learning Algorithms: Revolutionizing AI in 2024

Machine learning (ML) has been the driving force behind many of the most groundbreaking AI advancements over the past decade. However, 2024 marks a new chapter in ML's evolution, as enhanced algorithms push the boundaries of what machines can learn and accomplish. This chapter explores the development and impact of these enhanced machine learning algorithms, focusing on their contributions to precision, scalability, and versatility across industries.

From Traditional ML to Enhanced Algorithms

Traditional machine learning algorithms, such as decision trees, support vector machines, and basic neural networks, laid the foundation for AI's early successes. These algorithms allowed machines to analyze data, identify patterns, and make predictions, revolutionizing fields such as healthcare, finance, and marketing.

However, as the complexity of data increased and the demand for more accurate and reliable models grew, the limitations of these traditional algorithms became apparent. In response, enhanced machine learning algorithms began to emerge, addressing the need for greater efficiency, scalability, and precision. These next-generation algorithms incorporate innovations such as deep learning, reinforcement learning, and transfer learning to achieve superior results.

Key Innovations in Enhanced Machine Learning Algorithms

Deep Learning and Neural Networks
Deep learning, a subset of machine learning, has been at the forefront of AI's evolution. In 2024, deep learning algorithms have become even more powerful with innovations in architecture and training methods.

Transformer Models: Introduced in the late 2010s, transformer models revolutionized natural language processing (NLP) by allowing machines to understand and generate human language more effectively. In 2024, enhanced transformer models, such as GPT-4 and beyond, have further improved language understanding, enabling AI systems to handle more complex tasks such as translation, summarization, and conversational AI.

Self-Supervised Learning: Traditional deep learning algorithms often required large labeled datasets for training, which limited their applicability in areas where labeled data is scarce. However, self-supervised learning (SSL) has gained prominence in 2024, allowing models to learn useful representations from vast amounts of unlabeled data. This approach has dramatically reduced the need for manual data labeling and expanded the reach of machine learning into domains where data is unstructured or difficult to annotate.

Reinforcement Learning and Autonomous Systems
Reinforcement learning (RL) has seen significant advancements in 2024, particularly in the realm of autonomous systems. RL algorithms enable machines to learn through trial and error by interacting with their environments and receiving feedback in the form of rewards or penalties.

Model-Free RL: One of the major breakthroughs in 2024 is the refinement of model-free reinforcement learning algorithms. These algorithms do not rely on a predefined model of the environment but instead learn optimal behaviors through repeated interactions. This has enabled the development of more sophisticated autonomous agents, from self-driving cars to AI-powered robots in manufacturing, capable of adapting to dynamic and unpredictable environments.

Hierarchical RL: Another enhancement in 2024 is the rise of hierarchical reinforcement learning, where complex tasks are broken down into subtasks that can be learned and optimized individually. This has significantly improved the scalability and efficiency of RL algorithms, making them more practical for real-world applications.

Transfer Learning and Domain Adaptation
Transfer learning has become a crucial tool for enhancing machine learning algorithms, particularly in 2024 as models are required to perform well across different domains and tasks.

Few-Shot Learning: Transfer learning enables models to leverage knowledge from one domain and apply it to another, significantly reducing the amount of training data needed for new tasks. Few-shot learning, a variant of transfer learning, has become increasingly important in 2024, allowing models to learn new concepts with minimal data. This has been particularly useful in specialized industries like healthcare, where labeled data is limited and expensive to obtain.

Domain Adaptation: Enhanced machine learning algorithms in 2024 are also better equipped to handle domain adaptation, where models trained in one domain (e.g., medical imaging) can be adapted to perform well in a related but distinct domain (e.g., satellite imagery). This flexibility has expanded the applicability of ML across a broader range of industries and applications.

Federated Learning and Privacy-Preserving AI
In an era of heightened data privacy concerns, 2024 has

seen significant advancements in federated learning—a machine learning technique that allows models to be trained across decentralized data sources without requiring the data to be shared or centralized.

Federated Learning for Healthcare: In healthcare, where data privacy is paramount, federated learning has enabled hospitals and research institutions to collaboratively train AI models on patient data without compromising privacy. This has accelerated the development of predictive models for personalized medicine, early disease detection, and clinical decision support.

Differential Privacy: Alongside federated learning, differential privacy techniques have been enhanced in 2024 to ensure that individual data points cannot be identified or extracted from a trained model. This has strengthened the trustworthiness of AI systems, particularly in sectors like finance and government, where data security is critical.

Graph Neural Networks and Complex Data Structures One of the most promising innovations in enhanced machine learning algorithms is the development of graph neural networks (GNNs), which have become widely adopted in 2024 due to their ability to model complex relationships and dependencies in data.

Applications in Biology and Chemistry: GNNs are particularly well-suited for tasks that involve intricate data structures, such as molecular analysis in biology and chemistry. In 2024, GNNs have played a key role in drug discovery by modeling the interactions between molecules and predicting their properties, accelerating the development of new therapeutics.

Social Network Analysis: GNNs have also been used extensively in social network analysis, where they can model relationships between individuals, groups, and organizations. Enhanced GNN algorithms in 2024 allow companies to analyze social dynamics, identify influential nodes in a network, and predict the spread of information or behavior.

Real-World Applications of Enhanced ML Algorithms

The advancements in machine learning algorithms in 2024 have unlocked new possibilities across a wide range of industries:

Healthcare: Enhanced ML algorithms are being used for early detection of diseases, personalized treatment recommendations, and AI-assisted surgery. Predictive models trained with federated learning are helping hospitals improve patient outcomes while ensuring data privacy.

Finance: AI-driven algorithms in finance are analyzing market trends, predicting stock movements, and optimizing investment strategies. Enhanced algorithms for fraud detection and risk management are reducing financial losses and increasing security.

Energy: In the energy sector, enhanced ML algorithms are optimizing the operation of renewable energy sources, predicting energy demand, and improving grid management. AI-powered solutions are playing a key role in reducing carbon footprints and driving the transition to sustainable energy.

Transportation: Autonomous vehicles rely on sophisticated reinforcement learning algorithms to navigate complex environments, respond to dynamic traffic conditions, and make real-time decisions. Enhanced ML models are improving the safety and reliability of self-driving cars, drones, and delivery robots.

Challenges and Future Directions

While the enhanced machine learning algorithms of 2024 represent significant progress, challenges remain:

Data Bias: Ensuring that algorithms are trained on diverse and representative datasets is critical to avoiding biased outcomes. In 2024, there is increasing attention to fairness and inclusivity in AI, but addressing bias remains an ongoing challenge.

Explainability: As machine learning models become more complex, understanding how they make decisions becomes more difficult. The need for explainable AI (XAI) is growing, particularly in high-stakes areas like healthcare and finance, where transparency is essential.

Energy Consumption: Training large-scale machine learning models, particularly deep learning algorithms, requires significant computational resources and energy. In 2024, researchers are focused on developing more energy-efficient algorithms and exploring alternative approaches, such as quantum computing, to reduce the environmental impact of AI.

The enhanced machine learning algorithms of 2024 have revolutionized the AI landscape, driving innovation across industries and unlocking new possibilities for automation, discovery, and decision-making. From deep learning advancements to privacy-preserving AI and graph neural networks, these algorithms are pushing the boundaries of what AI can achieve. As AI continues to evolve, the focus will shift toward ensuring that these technologies are ethical, transparent, and sustainable, shaping a future where AI plays a central role in solving the world's most pressing challenges.

AI-Driven Automation and Efficiency: Transforming Industries in 2024

In 2024, AI-driven automation has become a pivotal force reshaping industries and unlocking unprecedented levels of efficiency. As businesses strive to remain competitive in a rapidly evolving digital landscape, the integration of artificial intelligence (AI) into workflows, production lines, and decision-making processes has led to transformative changes. From manufacturing and logistics to finance and healthcare, AI-driven automation is streamlining operations, reducing costs, and enabling organizations to achieve more with fewer resources.

This chapter explores the critical role of AI-driven automation in enhancing efficiency, the technologies powering this revolution, and the real-world applications that are redefining industry standards.

The Evolution of AI-Driven Automation

Automation, in its earlier forms, was primarily concerned with repetitive, rule-based tasks. Machines and algorithms could follow predefined instructions to complete tasks faster and more accurately than humans. However, the rise of AI has elevated automation to new heights. Unlike traditional automation, AI-driven automation is capable of learning from data, adapting to new situations, and making intelligent decisions with minimal human intervention.

In 2024, several key technologies have driven the rise of AI-driven automation:

Machine Learning (ML) and Deep Learning
Machine learning algorithms power many AI-driven automation systems by enabling machines to learn patterns from vast amounts of data. Deep learning, a subset of machine learning, allows AI models to handle unstructured data like images, videos, and natural language. These capabilities have broadened the scope of automation beyond rule-based processes, allowing AI systems to automate more complex and creative tasks.

Robotic Process Automation (RPA) with AI
Robotic process automation (RPA) has been around for years, but in 2024, it has become much more powerful when combined with AI. Traditional RPA systems automate routine, repetitive tasks by mimicking human interactions with software. However, AI-powered RPA systems, often referred to as **intelligent automation**, can handle unstructured data, learn from mistakes, and make decisions based on real-time insights. This has expanded the scope of automation to include tasks like customer service, financial reporting, and fraud detection.

Natural Language Processing (NLP) and Conversational AI

AI-driven automation has made significant strides in customer service, thanks to advancements in natural language processing (NLP) and conversational AI. In 2024, AI-powered chatbots and virtual assistants can understand and respond to customer queries with a high level of accuracy, providing instant support without the need for human agents. These systems can also handle more complex conversations, driving improvements in customer experience and operational efficiency.

Autonomous Systems and Robotics

In industries like manufacturing, logistics, and transportation, autonomous systems are becoming more prevalent. AI-driven robots, drones, and autonomous vehicles are capable of operating with minimal human supervision, optimizing production lines, managing inventory, and delivering goods. In 2024, these systems have become more adaptable and intelligent, capable of handling unpredictable environments and making real-time decisions based on sensor data and AI algorithms.

Efficiency Gains Across Industries

AI-driven automation has revolutionized efficiency across a range of industries in 2024, enabling organizations to optimize their operations, reduce costs, and enhance productivity. Here's how AI is reshaping key sectors:

Manufacturing and Industrial Automation

In manufacturing, AI-driven automation has led to the rise of the "smart factory," where machines, robots, and AI systems work together to streamline production processes. With AI-powered sensors and predictive analytics, factories can monitor machinery in real time, detect potential issues before they cause downtime, and optimize workflows for maximum efficiency.

Predictive Maintenance: One of the most significant applications of AI in manufacturing is predictive maintenance. AI systems analyze sensor data from equipment to predict when a machine is likely to fail, allowing maintenance teams to intervene before a breakdown occurs. This has dramatically reduced downtime, improved equipment lifespan, and lowered maintenance costs.

Automated Quality Control: AI-powered visual inspection systems use machine learning algorithms to detect defects in products during the manufacturing process. These systems can identify even the smallest imperfections with high accuracy, improving product quality and reducing waste.

Logistics and Supply Chain Management
AI-driven automation is transforming logistics and supply chain management, enhancing efficiency by optimizing routes, managing inventory, and predicting demand.

Autonomous Vehicles and Drones: In 2024, AI-powered autonomous vehicles and drones are increasingly being used for deliveries. These systems can optimize routes in real time based on traffic and weather conditions, reducing delivery times and costs. Autonomous warehouses, where AI-driven robots manage inventory, pack orders, and load trucks, are becoming more common, further streamlining logistics operations.

Demand Forecasting and Inventory Management: AI systems can analyze historical sales data, market trends, and external factors such as weather to predict demand with greater accuracy. This allows companies to optimize their inventory levels, ensuring that they have the right amount of stock without overordering or understocking. AI-driven demand forecasting has reduced costs and improved customer satisfaction by ensuring timely deliveries.

Healthcare
AI-driven automation is making healthcare more efficient by automating administrative tasks, improving diagnostics, and enabling personalized medicine.

AI-Powered Diagnostics: AI algorithms are now being used to analyze medical images, such as X-rays and MRIs, to detect conditions like cancer and heart disease. These systems can often identify abnormalities more quickly and accurately than human radiologists, allowing for earlier diagnosis and treatment.

Automated Administrative Tasks: In healthcare, many time-consuming administrative tasks, such as scheduling, billing, and patient record management, are being automated with AI. Virtual assistants and chatbots are handling appointment scheduling and answering patient queries, freeing up healthcare staff to focus on more critical tasks.

Robotic Surgery: AI-powered surgical robots are performing minimally invasive surgeries with greater precision, reducing recovery times and improving patient outcomes. In 2024, advancements in AI-driven robotic surgery have expanded the range of procedures that can be performed autonomously or with minimal human assistance.

Finance
AI-driven automation is revolutionizing the financial services sector by automating processes such as risk management, fraud detection, and customer service.

Fraud Detection: AI-powered systems analyze transaction data in real time to detect patterns indicative of fraudulent activity. By continuously learning from new data, these systems are becoming more effective at identifying suspicious behavior, helping financial institutions prevent fraud and minimize losses.

Automated Trading: In financial markets, AI algorithms are being used to execute trades at speeds far beyond human capability. These systems analyze vast amounts of data in real time, allowing them to identify trading opportunities and execute transactions at optimal prices. Automated trading has improved market liquidity and reduced transaction costs.

AI-Enhanced Customer Service: Banks and financial institutions are using AI-powered chatbots to handle customer inquiries, resolve issues, and provide personalized financial advice. These systems are capable of understanding natural language, offering instant support to customers without the need for human intervention.

Challenges and Considerations

While AI-driven automation is unlocking significant efficiency gains, it also presents several challenges that organizations must address in 2024:

Workforce Displacement and Reskilling

As AI-driven automation takes over routine tasks, there are concerns about job displacement in various industries. While automation improves efficiency, it can lead to the reduction of certain roles, particularly in manufacturing, logistics, and administrative positions. However, forward-thinking companies are investing in reskilling programs to help workers transition into new roles that require more advanced skills, such as AI system management, data analysis, and strategic decision-making.

Data Security and Privacy

AI-driven automation relies heavily on data, raising concerns about data security and privacy. Automated systems handle sensitive information in industries like healthcare and finance, making it essential to implement robust security measures. Additionally, organizations must ensure compliance with data privacy regulations, such as GDPR, to protect personal information.

AI Ethics and Transparency

As AI-driven automation becomes more widespread, questions about the ethical implications of AI decisions are gaining prominence. Organizations need to ensure that their AI systems are transparent, fair, and free from bias. In 2024, there is growing pressure on companies to adopt ethical AI practices, particularly in areas like hiring, lending, and law enforcement, where AI decisions can have significant consequences.

The Future of AI-Driven Automation

Looking beyond 2024, the role of AI-driven automation will continue to expand as new technologies emerge and businesses seek to further optimize their operations. The integration of AI with quantum computing, edge computing, and 5G networks will unlock new possibilities for real-time automation and decision-making. As AI systems become more intelligent, autonomous, and scalable, industries will experience even greater levels of efficiency, productivity, and innovation.

In 2024, AI-driven automation is at the forefront of a global efficiency revolution, transforming industries from manufacturing to healthcare. By streamlining processes, reducing costs, and improving decision-making, AI-powered systems are reshaping the way businesses operate. While challenges such as workforce displacement, data security, and ethical considerations remain, the benefits of AI-driven automation far outweigh the risks, positioning AI as a critical driver of efficiency and innovation in the years to come.

Advancements in Natural Language Processing (NLP): 2024 and Beyond

Natural Language Processing (NLP), a branch of artificial intelligence, has seen remarkable advancements in 2024, reshaping the way humans interact with machines. NLP enables machines to understand, interpret, and generate human language, allowing for seamless communication between people and technology. The rapid growth in this field has led to significant breakthroughs in applications ranging from virtual assistants and chatbots to language translation and content generation. In this chapter, we explore the latest advancements in NLP, their impact across various industries, and the future potential of this transformative technology.

The Evolution of NLP in 2024

NLP has come a long way from its early days, where simple rule-based systems attempted to interpret human language. Today, powered by deep learning and machine learning algorithms, NLP systems can comprehend the complexities of natural language, capturing context, sentiment, and even subtle nuances such as tone and intent. Several key innovations have contributed to this evolution in 2024:

Transformers and Large Language Models (LLMs)

The development of transformer-based architectures, such as OpenAI's GPT and Google's BERT, has revolutionized NLP by enabling more sophisticated language understanding and generation. These models can process massive datasets, learning patterns and relationships in language, which allows them to perform a wide range of tasks such as summarization, translation, and question-answering with human-like proficiency.

In 2024, the next generation of large language models (LLMs) has taken NLP to new heights, with models becoming more efficient, adaptable, and contextually aware. These models are capable of understanding the subtleties of language, including idioms, slang, and complex sentence structures, making their outputs more natural and coherent than ever before.

Multilingual NLP

Language barriers have long been a challenge in global communication, but in 2024, multilingual NLP systems are breaking down these barriers with unprecedented accuracy. Advancements in neural machine translation (NMT) have led to the development of multilingual models capable of translating between hundreds of languages without sacrificing quality. These systems can also generate translations that capture cultural nuances, making them more contextually relevant and reducing the risk of misinterpretation.

Moreover, NLP systems are now being trained on multilingual datasets, allowing them to perform tasks such as sentiment analysis and text classification across multiple languages without the need for language-specific models. This has opened up new possibilities for businesses and organizations seeking to reach global audiences.

Conversational AI and Virtual Assistants

Conversational AI, powered by NLP, has made significant strides in 2024, enabling virtual assistants and chatbots to engage in more natural, context-aware conversations. Unlike earlier versions that relied on predefined responses, today's systems can understand and generate language in real-time, adapting to the user's input and providing more personalized, human-like interactions.

These advancements are particularly evident in customer service, where AI-powered virtual assistants can now handle complex queries, offer personalized recommendations, and even understand emotional cues through sentiment analysis. The use of NLP-driven chatbots is becoming standard in industries like e-commerce, banking, and healthcare, where they provide efficient, 24/7 support to customers.

Zero-Shot and Few-Shot Learning

Traditional NLP systems often require large amounts of

labeled data to perform well on specific tasks, but in 2024, zero-shot and few-shot learning have changed this paradigm. These techniques allow NLP models to generalize from a limited number of examples (few-shot) or even none (zero-shot), enabling them to perform new tasks without requiring extensive retraining.

This advancement has made NLP more versatile and cost-effective, as models can now be applied to new domains and tasks with minimal data, reducing the need for labor-intensive annotation processes. In particular, this has benefited industries such as healthcare, where labeled datasets are scarce or costly to produce.

Contextual and Sentiment-Aware NLP

One of the key breakthroughs in 2024 is the ability of NLP systems to understand context at a deeper level. Models are now capable of recognizing not only the meaning of words and phrases but also their context within a broader conversation or document. This enables more accurate sentiment analysis, where NLP systems can detect underlying emotions, sarcasm, and intent, allowing for more nuanced interactions and insights.

For instance, businesses are using sentiment-aware NLP to monitor customer feedback on social media, identifying shifts in public opinion and proactively addressing potential issues. Similarly, sentiment analysis is being applied in healthcare to assess patient well-being and in finance to gauge market sentiment.

Applications of Advanced NLP in 2024

NLP's advancements are being leveraged across numerous sectors, transforming industries and redefining the way we interact with information. Some key applications of NLP in 2024 include:

Healthcare

NLP is playing a vital role in the healthcare industry, improving clinical documentation, automating administrative tasks, and enabling more personalized patient care. AI-powered NLP systems can extract relevant information from unstructured clinical notes, streamlining the process of medical coding and billing. They can also assist in diagnosing conditions by analyzing patient data and medical records.
Moreover, conversational AI is enhancing telemedicine services, allowing patients to interact with virtual assistants that can understand and respond to their concerns in natural language. These assistants can provide medical advice, schedule appointments, and help patients manage their health conditions, all while reducing the burden on healthcare professionals.

Legal and Regulatory Compliance

The legal industry is benefiting from NLP's ability to process vast amounts of text and extract meaningful insights. In 2024, NLP systems are being used to analyze contracts, legal documents, and regulatory guidelines, helping organizations ensure compliance and identify potential risks. NLP models can quickly flag clauses or terms that deviate from standard practices, allowing legal teams to focus on more complex, high-value tasks.

Additionally, NLP-driven systems are aiding in e-discovery, where AI can sift through large datasets of emails, documents, and other digital records to identify relevant information in legal cases. This not only speeds up the process but also reduces costs associated with manual review.

Content Generation and Summarization

With the advancements in large language models, NLP is now capable of generating high-quality content at scale. In 2024, businesses are using AI-powered content generation tools to create product descriptions, blog posts, and marketing copy that resonate with their target audiences. These systems can also summarize lengthy documents, extracting key information and presenting it in a concise, digestible format.

In journalism, NLP is being used to automate the generation of news articles, particularly in data-heavy domains like finance and sports. AI-driven tools can analyze financial reports or match statistics, generating well-structured articles in real-time. This allows media outlets to deliver news faster while freeing up human journalists to focus on investigative reporting and in-depth analysis.

Language Translation and Global Communication
Advancements in multilingual NLP have made real-time translation more accurate and accessible than ever before. In 2024, NLP-powered translation tools are enabling seamless communication between people who speak different languages, whether in business meetings, travel, or online interactions. These tools can handle not only written text but also spoken language, providing real-time voice translation with a high degree of accuracy.
NLP-driven translation systems are also being integrated into customer service platforms, allowing companies to provide support in multiple languages without the need for human translators. This has opened up new markets for businesses, enabling them to reach global audiences and deliver a more personalized customer experience.

Education and E-Learning
In the field of education, NLP is being used to create intelligent tutoring systems that can adapt to individual student needs. These systems can assess a student's understanding of a topic based on their language inputs

and provide personalized feedback to improve learning outcomes. Additionally, NLP is being used to develop tools that assist in language learning by analyzing speech and writing, offering real-time corrections, and suggesting improvements.

NLP-powered educational platforms are also helping teachers by automating grading and feedback on assignments, saving time and allowing them to focus on more critical aspects of instruction. In 2024, these platforms are making education more accessible and personalized, improving student engagement and success.

Challenges and Ethical Considerations

While NLP has made remarkable progress, several challenges and ethical considerations remain:

Bias in NLP Models

One of the ongoing challenges in NLP is the issue of bias. Since NLP models are trained on large datasets that reflect human language, they can inadvertently learn and perpetuate biases present in the data. In 2024, researchers are working on methods to detect and mitigate these biases, ensuring that NLP systems make fair and unbiased decisions, particularly in sensitive areas like hiring, lending, and law enforcement.

Data Privacy and Security

NLP systems often require access to vast amounts of data, including sensitive personal information. Ensuring the privacy and security of this data is a significant concern, particularly in industries like healthcare and finance. Organizations must implement robust security measures and comply with data protection regulations to safeguard user data while benefiting from NLP's capabilities.

Interpretability and Transparency

As NLP models become more complex, it becomes increasingly difficult to understand how they arrive at certain decisions or outputs. This lack of transparency can be problematic, especially in critical applications such as healthcare or legal decision-making. In 2024, there is a growing focus on developing explainable NLP systems that provide insights into how they process language and make decisions.

The Future of NLP

Looking ahead, NLP is poised to continue its rapid evolution, with several exciting developments on the horizon:

Real-Time, Multimodal NLP

Future NLP systems will be capable of understanding and processing not only text but also other forms of data, such as images, videos, and speech. Multimodal NLP will enable more seamless interactions between humans and machines, allowing AI systems to interpret and respond to complex, real-world inputs in real-time.

Personalized NLP Models
As NLP systems become more advanced, they will be able to tailor their outputs to individual users, taking into account their preferences, communication styles, and past interactions. Personalized NLP will enhance user experiences in applications such as virtual assistants, customer support, and content generation.

NLP for Knowledge Discovery
In the future, NLP will play a critical role in knowledge discovery, helping researchers and businesses extract valuable insights from vast amounts of unstructured data. Advanced NLP models will be able to autonomously analyze scientific papers, legal documents, and other sources of information, identifying patterns and relationships that were previously difficult to uncover.

The advancements in Natural Language Processing in 2024 have reshaped the way we interact with technology and opened up new possibilities across a wide range of industries. From improving customer experiences and automating content generation to enabling real-time, multilingual communication, NLP is transforming the digital landscape. While challenges remain, the future of NLP promises even greater innovation, pushing the boundaries of what machines can understand and achieve with human language.

AI in Cybersecurity: Threat Detection and Prevention

In 2024, the integration of artificial intelligence (AI) into cybersecurity has transformed the way organizations detect and prevent threats. With the ever-increasing complexity and volume of cyberattacks, traditional methods of defense are no longer sufficient to protect sensitive data and critical infrastructure. AI-driven solutions are now at the forefront of cybersecurity, providing real-time, adaptive, and scalable defenses that can outpace and outsmart cybercriminals. This chapter explores how AI is revolutionizing threat detection and prevention, the key technologies behind it, and the challenges that come with this evolving landscape.

The Cyber Threat Landscape in 2024

The modern cyber threat landscape is characterized by sophisticated attacks targeting businesses, governments, and individuals alike. From ransomware and phishing to zero-day exploits and state-sponsored hacking, the variety and scale of cyber threats have expanded dramatically. In response, cybersecurity teams are increasingly turning to AI to bolster their defenses and stay ahead of adversaries. The main drivers behind AI's rise in cybersecurity include:

Proliferation of Cyber Threats

Cyberattacks have become more frequent and complex, with malicious actors utilizing AI to automate their efforts. AI enables attackers to develop advanced malware that can adapt, learn, and evade traditional security measures. In 2024, cybersecurity teams must defend against AI-enhanced threats such as polymorphic malware, which changes its code to avoid detection, and AI-driven phishing campaigns that craft convincing social engineering attacks.

Data Overload and Limited Human Resources

The sheer volume of security data generated by modern networks is overwhelming for human analysts. Security Information and Event Management (SIEM) systems, firewalls, intrusion detection systems (IDS), and endpoint detection and response (EDR) tools produce vast amounts of logs and alerts. Sorting through this data to identify genuine threats is a monumental task. AI excels in processing large datasets quickly and accurately, allowing security teams to focus on high-priority incidents.

Need for Real-Time Responses

Traditional cybersecurity solutions often rely on manual intervention and rule-based systems, which can be slow and reactive. As cyberattacks become more automated and fast-moving, organizations need AI-powered solutions that can detect and respond to threats in real-time, minimizing damage and reducing downtime.

AI-Driven Threat Detection

AI's ability to detect threats is rooted in its capacity to learn from data and recognize patterns that indicate malicious behavior. The primary technologies behind AI-driven threat detection include:

Machine Learning (ML) for Anomaly Detection
Machine learning models are adept at identifying abnormal behavior in network traffic, user activity, and system processes. By training on historical data, ML algorithms can learn what constitutes "normal" activity within an organization's network and flag deviations that may indicate a security breach. This approach is particularly effective in detecting unknown or zero-day attacks that do not match any existing signatures.
For example, AI can monitor user behavior for signs of credential theft or insider threats by recognizing unusual login times, access to sensitive data, or anomalous patterns in file usage. AI-based anomaly detection systems are also used to spot abnormal network traffic, which may indicate an intrusion, data exfiltration, or the presence of malware.

Natural Language Processing (NLP) for Phishing Detection

AI's advancements in natural language processing (NLP) have enabled more sophisticated detection of phishing emails and fraudulent communications. Phishing remains one of the most common attack vectors, and traditional spam filters often struggle to keep up with increasingly personalized and convincing phishing attempts.

In 2024, AI-driven solutions use NLP to analyze the content, tone, and structure of emails to detect signs of phishing. These systems can also assess the behavior of the sender and analyze email headers and metadata to flag suspicious messages. Moreover, AI tools are being used to train employees by simulating phishing attacks, helping to raise awareness and reduce the likelihood of successful phishing attempts.

Behavioral Analytics for Endpoint Protection

AI-powered behavioral analytics enhance endpoint security by continuously monitoring the behavior of devices, applications, and users. Instead of relying solely on signature-based detection methods, AI systems can recognize patterns of behavior that suggest malicious intent. This approach helps to detect fileless malware, advanced persistent threats (APTs), and other sophisticated attacks that evade traditional antivirus solutions.

AI-driven endpoint protection platforms (EPPs) can also predict potential threats by analyzing system behavior in real-time, isolating suspicious processes before they can cause harm. For example, if an endpoint begins executing abnormal system commands or accessing unusual files, AI can flag and contain the activity before it results in a breach.

AI in Intrusion Detection and Prevention Systems (IDPS)
AI is transforming Intrusion Detection and Prevention Systems (IDPS) by enabling more accurate detection and proactive defense mechanisms. AI-driven IDPS can process vast amounts of network data to identify potential threats more quickly than traditional systems. They are capable of detecting not only known attack patterns but also emerging threats that do not yet have known signatures.

With AI, IDPS can adapt to evolving threats by learning from previous attacks and adjusting detection parameters in real-time. Additionally, AI enhances the ability of IDPS to identify false positives, reducing the burden on security teams and allowing them to focus on genuine threats.

AI-Powered Threat Prevention

While threat detection is critical, AI's role in preventing attacks is equally important. AI-powered cybersecurity solutions proactively defend against threats by:

Predictive Security Analytics

Predictive analytics, powered by AI, enables organizations to anticipate and prevent cyberattacks before they occur. By analyzing historical data, current threat intelligence, and known attack patterns, AI models can predict potential vulnerabilities and recommend preemptive actions. This proactive approach helps organizations strengthen their defenses, patch vulnerabilities, and implement stronger security protocols in anticipation of future threats.

Automated Incident Response

In 2024, AI is playing a significant role in automating incident response, reducing the time it takes to detect, investigate, and mitigate threats. AI-driven Security Orchestration, Automation, and Response (SOAR) platforms can automatically triage alerts, correlate them with threat intelligence, and initiate predefined responses without the need for human intervention. For instance, if AI detects a ransomware attack, it can automatically isolate affected systems, block further communication, and initiate data recovery processes. This swift response minimizes the impact of the attack and reduces the need for manual intervention, allowing security teams to focus on more strategic tasks.

Threat Intelligence Integration
AI-powered cybersecurity solutions can integrate real-time threat intelligence from multiple sources, including external databases, dark web monitoring, and industry reports. This enables organizations to stay up-to-date with the latest threat trends and adjust their defenses accordingly. By correlating threat intelligence with internal security data, AI systems can prioritize alerts and prevent attacks by identifying and neutralizing emerging threats before they become critical.
For example, AI-driven threat intelligence platforms can identify potential vulnerabilities in an organization's software stack by analyzing recent security advisories, enabling the organization to patch the issue before it is exploited.

Deception Technology
Deception technology, powered by AI, is an emerging method of threat prevention that involves creating fake assets or environments (decoys) to lure attackers and gather intelligence on their tactics. AI enables these decoys to mimic real systems more convincingly, tricking attackers into engaging with the fake environment while the real systems remain secure.
By analyzing how attackers interact with decoys, AI can provide valuable insights into attack techniques and

alert security teams to potential vulnerabilities. This proactive defense strategy helps organizations stay ahead of attackers and respond more effectively to future threats.

Challenges and Limitations

While AI has greatly enhanced cybersecurity capabilities, several challenges and limitations persist:

Adversarial AI

Cybercriminals are increasingly using AI to improve their attacks, creating a constant arms race between defenders and adversaries. AI-generated phishing emails, automated malware, and deepfake attacks are just a few examples of how attackers are leveraging AI to bypass security measures. Defending against AI-driven attacks requires continuous innovation and investment in advanced AI-powered defenses.

False Positives and Model Interpretability

One of the challenges of AI in cybersecurity is the potential for false positives, where legitimate activity is flagged as suspicious. While AI can reduce the number of false positives, they still occur, especially in highly dynamic environments. Furthermore, the black-box nature of some AI models makes it difficult to understand why a particular decision was made, complicating efforts to fine-tune the system or explain its findings to stakeholders.

Data Privacy and Ethical Concerns
AI-driven cybersecurity solutions often require access to large amounts of data to function effectively, raising concerns about data privacy and ethical considerations. Organizations must ensure that their use of AI complies with data protection regulations such as GDPR and CCPA while balancing the need for effective threat detection and prevention.

AI has become a cornerstone of modern cybersecurity, providing organizations with the tools they need to detect and prevent an ever-growing array of cyber threats. From machine learning-based anomaly detection and NLP-driven phishing prevention to automated incident response and predictive analytics, AI is transforming the way security teams defend against attacks. However, the arms race between AI-powered defenses and AI-driven threats is far from over. To stay ahead, organizations must continue to innovate, invest in advanced AI technologies, and address the ethical challenges that come with their use. As the threat landscape continues to evolve, AI will play an increasingly critical role in securing the digital world.

Streamlining Operations with AI-Powered Automation

AI-powered automation is revolutionizing how businesses operate in 2024, offering the ability to streamline processes, reduce operational costs, and improve overall efficiency. By automating repetitive tasks, enhancing decision-making, and driving innovation across industries, AI is enabling organizations to achieve greater productivity while focusing on strategic growth initiatives. This chapter explores the role of AI-driven automation in transforming business operations, the key technologies driving this change, and the impact on various sectors.

AI's Role in Automating Operations

AI-powered automation leverages machine learning (ML), natural language processing (NLP), and robotic process automation (RPA) to perform tasks traditionally handled by human workers. This combination of AI technologies allows businesses to automate complex, multi-step processes that require decision-making, pattern recognition, and data analysis.

Automating Repetitive and Routine Tasks

One of the most significant benefits of AI automation is its ability to handle repetitive, time-consuming tasks, freeing up human employees to focus on higher-value activities. From managing invoices and processing payroll to scheduling appointments and handling customer inquiries, AI-powered tools can perform routine operations faster and more accurately than humans.

For example, AI-driven RPA tools can automate the onboarding process for new employees, ensuring that forms are completed, accounts are set up, and necessary documentation is processed—all without manual intervention. Similarly, AI-powered chatbots can handle customer support queries, providing instant responses to common questions while escalating more complex issues to human agents.

AI for Predictive Maintenance and Monitoring

In sectors such as manufacturing, energy, and logistics, AI-powered automation is enhancing operations through predictive maintenance and monitoring. AI systems analyze data from sensors and machinery to predict when equipment is likely to fail, allowing organizations to perform maintenance before issues arise. This approach reduces costly downtime, extends the lifespan of machinery, and improves overall operational efficiency.

Predictive maintenance powered by AI can also help companies optimize their supply chain by automating inventory management and forecasting demand more accurately. AI can analyze historical data, current market trends, and real-time conditions to predict stock levels, reducing waste and ensuring that supply meets demand.

Automating Data Processing and Analysis

Businesses generate and collect vast amounts of data daily, but analyzing that data manually is often inefficient and prone to error. AI-powered automation allows organizations to process, organize, and analyze data quickly, uncovering insights that inform decision-making. Automated data analysis can help businesses spot trends, optimize performance, and make data-driven decisions.

In financial services, for example, AI tools can analyze transactions in real-time to detect fraudulent activity, flagging suspicious behavior that requires further investigation. Similarly, AI-powered analytics platforms in healthcare can process patient data to identify potential risks and recommend personalized treatments, improving patient outcomes while reducing administrative workloads.

AI-Driven Workflow Optimization

AI is also being used to streamline and optimize workflows by automating decision-making processes. By analyzing workflow data, AI systems can identify bottlenecks, suggest improvements, and automate key decisions, allowing organizations to operate more efficiently. This is particularly beneficial in sectors like finance, where AI can automate underwriting processes, loan approvals, and credit risk assessments based on a range of data inputs.

In project management, AI-powered platforms are used to optimize task allocation, ensuring that projects stay on track by identifying resource constraints and redistributing workloads. AI tools can provide real-time updates on project progress, predict potential delays, and suggest adjustments to meet deadlines.

Key Technologies Driving AI Automation

The advancements in AI-driven automation are powered by several key technologies:

Robotic Process Automation (RPA)
RPA enables organizations to automate routine tasks by mimicking human actions within digital systems. It is particularly effective for automating back-office operations, such as data entry, billing, and compliance reporting. AI-enhanced RPA takes automation to the next level by incorporating machine learning and decision-making capabilities, allowing systems to handle more complex tasks.

Machine Learning (ML)
ML algorithms enable AI systems to learn from data and improve their performance over time. In AI-powered

automation, ML is used to analyze patterns, predict outcomes, and make data-driven decisions. ML-driven automation is essential for applications such as predictive maintenance, fraud detection, and personalized marketing.

Natural Language Processing (NLP)

NLP allows AI systems to understand and interact with human language, making it possible to automate tasks such as customer service, content generation, and legal document analysis. AI chatbots and virtual assistants powered by NLP can handle customer interactions, answer questions, and process requests in real-time, reducing the need for human intervention.

Cognitive Automation

Cognitive automation refers to the integration of AI and RPA with cognitive technologies, such as image recognition and speech-to-text. This enables automation solutions to handle unstructured data, such as images, documents, and voice commands. Cognitive automation is used in industries like healthcare for automating medical image analysis and in finance for processing loan applications based on voice interactions.

Industry Applications of AI Automation

AI-powered automation is being adopted across a wide range of industries, transforming operations in unique ways.

Manufacturing
In manufacturing, AI automation enhances productivity by optimizing production lines, reducing downtime through predictive maintenance, and improving quality control. AI-powered robots can perform repetitive tasks, such as assembly and inspection, while AI systems analyze sensor data to prevent equipment failures. Automation is also driving innovation in smart factories, where AI controls and optimizes the entire production process in real-time.

Healthcare
AI automation in healthcare is revolutionizing administrative tasks, such as scheduling, billing, and patient data management, allowing healthcare providers to focus on patient care. AI-powered systems can analyze patient records to recommend treatments, automate diagnostic processes, and improve accuracy in medical imaging. Additionally, AI virtual assistants can help patients manage their health by providing personalized advice and reminders.

Financial Services

In finance, AI-driven automation is streamlining operations in areas such as fraud detection, loan processing, and wealth management. AI systems can analyze vast amounts of transaction data to detect suspicious activity in real-time, reducing the risk of fraud. Automated investment platforms, or robo-advisors, use AI to manage portfolios based on individual risk preferences, while AI-powered chatbots provide customer service for routine banking inquiries.

Retail

AI automation is transforming the retail industry by optimizing inventory management, enhancing customer experiences, and automating marketing campaigns. AI-driven recommendation engines analyze customer behavior to offer personalized product suggestions, while chatbots handle customer inquiries and assist with online purchases. Retailers are also using AI to automate logistics and supply chain operations, ensuring that stock levels are maintained, and orders are fulfilled quickly.

Energy and Utilities

In the energy sector, AI automation is improving grid management, optimizing energy consumption, and reducing operational costs. AI-powered systems can forecast energy demand, monitor equipment performance, and automate grid adjustments in response to real-time conditions. Automated systems are also helping utilities detect faults and prevent outages, improving overall service reliability.

Benefits of AI-Powered Automation

The adoption of AI-powered automation offers several significant benefits for organizations:

Increased Efficiency and Productivity
By automating repetitive and manual tasks, AI frees up human workers to focus on more complex and creative tasks. This boosts productivity and allows organizations to achieve more with fewer resources.

Cost Savings
Automating processes reduces the need for human labor, leading to cost savings in areas such as payroll, training, and benefits. AI-powered automation also minimizes the risk of errors and reduces operational inefficiencies, resulting in further cost reductions.

Improved Decision-Making
AI-driven automation enhances decision-making by providing real-time insights, analyzing large datasets, and predicting outcomes based on historical data. Organizations can make more informed, data-driven decisions that improve performance and reduce risks.

Scalability

AI-powered automation allows organizations to scale their operations without needing to increase headcount. Automated systems can handle large volumes of tasks and data, ensuring that operations run smoothly even as the business grows.

Challenges and Considerations

While AI-powered automation offers numerous benefits, there are also challenges that organizations must address:

Integration with Legacy Systems

Implementing AI automation often requires integration with existing legacy systems, which can be complex and costly. Organizations must invest in the necessary infrastructure and ensure that AI solutions can work seamlessly with their current technology stack.

Workforce Displacement

As AI automation takes over repetitive tasks, there is a risk of workforce displacement, particularly in industries heavily reliant on manual labor. Organizations must invest in retraining and reskilling employees to prepare them for new roles in a more automated environment.

Data Privacy and Security

AI systems require access to large amounts of data to function effectively, raising concerns about data privacy and security. Organizations must ensure that their AI automation tools comply with data protection regulations and implement robust security measures to prevent breaches.

AI-powered automation is reshaping the future of business operations, driving efficiency, reducing costs, and improving decision-making across industries. From automating routine tasks to optimizing complex workflows, AI is empowering organizations to achieve more with less, allowing them to focus on strategic growth. However, as AI automation continues to evolve, organizations must address challenges such as integration, workforce displacement, and data privacy to fully realize its potential. The future of operations lies in AI-driven automation, and those who embrace it will be well-positioned to succeed in an increasingly competitive landscape.

Predictive Analytics for Better Decision-Making

In today's fast-paced business environment, making informed decisions quickly is crucial for maintaining a competitive edge. Predictive analytics, fueled by advancements in artificial intelligence (AI) and machine learning (ML), offers organizations the ability to forecast future outcomes based on historical data and trends. By leveraging sophisticated algorithms, businesses can make data-driven decisions that improve performance, reduce risks, and capitalize on emerging opportunities. This chapter explores how predictive analytics is revolutionizing decision-making, the underlying technologies powering it, and its applications across various industries.

What is Predictive Analytics?

Predictive analytics involves the use of statistical techniques, machine learning algorithms, and data mining to analyze historical data and make predictions about future events. It allows organizations to identify patterns, forecast trends, and predict behavior, enabling them to make proactive decisions. Unlike traditional analytics, which provides insights based on past events, predictive analytics focuses on anticipating what will happen next.

By analyzing large datasets, predictive analytics can uncover correlations that may not be immediately visible to humans. These insights can be applied to various decision-making processes, from optimizing marketing strategies to improving supply chain management and mitigating financial risks.

How Predictive Analytics Works

The predictive analytics process involves several key steps:

Data Collection and Preprocessing
The foundation of predictive analytics is data. Organizations collect vast amounts of data from multiple sources, including internal databases, customer interactions, market trends, and external sensors. This raw data is then cleaned, processed, and prepared for analysis, ensuring that it is accurate, complete, and relevant.

Building Predictive Models
Once the data is prepared, machine learning algorithms are applied to create predictive models. These models are trained on historical data to identify patterns and relationships between different variables. The more data the model is exposed to, the better it becomes at making accurate predictions.

Testing and Validation

Predictive models are then tested and validated using a separate dataset to evaluate their accuracy. This step ensures that the models can generalize to new, unseen data and are not overfitted to the training set.

Generating Predictions

Once the model is validated, it can be used to generate predictions. Organizations can feed new data into the model to forecast future outcomes, such as customer behavior, sales trends, or equipment failures. The predictions provide actionable insights that help decision-makers plan for the future.

Continuous Improvement

Predictive analytics is an ongoing process. As new data becomes available, models are updated and refined to improve their accuracy and relevance. Machine learning algorithms allow predictive models to adapt to changing conditions and evolving trends, ensuring that predictions remain accurate over time.

Key Technologies Behind Predictive Analytics

Predictive analytics relies on several advanced technologies to deliver accurate and actionable insights:

Machine Learning (ML)

Machine learning algorithms are the driving force behind predictive analytics. These algorithms learn from data, identifying patterns and making predictions based on that information. Popular machine learning techniques for predictive analytics include decision trees, regression analysis, neural networks, and support vector machines (SVMs).

Big Data

The rise of big data has significantly enhanced the capabilities of predictive analytics. By analyzing vast datasets from multiple sources, organizations can gain deeper insights and make more accurate predictions. Big data technologies, such as Hadoop and Apache Spark, enable organizations to process and analyze large volumes of data quickly.

Artificial Intelligence (AI)

AI technologies, including deep learning and natural language processing (NLP), play a key role in predictive analytics by enabling models to learn and improve over time. AI allows predictive models to recognize complex patterns in unstructured data, such as text and images, providing even more accurate predictions.

Data Mining

Data mining techniques are used to discover hidden patterns within large datasets. By analyzing historical data, organizations can identify trends and relationships that inform predictive models. Data mining tools help extract valuable insights from structured and unstructured data, enabling better decision-making.

Applications of Predictive Analytics

Predictive analytics has applications across a wide range of industries, enabling organizations to optimize operations, reduce costs, and improve customer experiences.

Marketing and Customer Analytics

Predictive analytics is widely used in marketing to anticipate customer behavior and optimize marketing campaigns. By analyzing customer data, businesses can predict which products or services customers are likely to purchase, allowing them to target their marketing efforts more effectively. Predictive models can also forecast customer churn, enabling organizations to take proactive steps to retain valuable customers.

For example, online retailers use predictive analytics to recommend products based on customers' past purchases and browsing behavior. By offering personalized recommendations, businesses can increase conversion rates and customer satisfaction.

Supply Chain Optimization

Predictive analytics is transforming supply chain management by enabling organizations to forecast demand, optimize inventory levels, and reduce waste. By analyzing historical sales data and external factors such as market trends and weather patterns, businesses can predict demand fluctuations and adjust their supply chains accordingly.

This predictive capability helps companies minimize stockouts and overstock situations, improving operational efficiency and reducing costs. Additionally, predictive analytics can identify potential disruptions in the supply chain, allowing businesses to mitigate risks and ensure continuity.

Financial Risk Management

In the financial sector, predictive analytics is used to assess risk, detect fraud, and optimize investment strategies. By analyzing historical financial data, predictive models can forecast market trends, assess credit risk, and predict potential loan defaults. These insights enable financial institutions to make better decisions regarding lending, investments, and asset management.

Predictive analytics is also used in fraud detection, where it analyzes transaction data to identify suspicious behavior in real-time. By detecting patterns indicative of fraudulent activity, organizations can take preventive measures to protect their assets and reputation.

Healthcare and Patient Care

Predictive analytics is playing an increasingly important role in healthcare, helping providers deliver personalized care and improve patient outcomes. By analyzing patient data, predictive models can identify individuals at risk for chronic conditions, recommend preventive measures, and optimize treatment plans.

For instance, predictive analytics can forecast hospital admissions based on historical patient data, allowing healthcare providers to allocate resources more efficiently. It can also help identify potential complications during surgery, enabling doctors to take proactive steps to mitigate risks.

Manufacturing and Predictive Maintenance
Predictive analytics is revolutionizing the manufacturing industry by enabling predictive maintenance. By analyzing data from machinery and equipment, predictive models can forecast when equipment is likely to fail, allowing organizations to perform maintenance before a breakdown occurs.

This approach reduces costly downtime, extends the lifespan of machinery, and improves operational efficiency. Additionally, predictive analytics can optimize production processes by analyzing performance data and identifying areas for improvement.

Human Resources and Talent Management
In human resources, predictive analytics is used to improve talent acquisition, retention, and employee performance. By analyzing data on employee behavior, performance, and engagement, organizations can

predict which employees are likely to leave and take steps to retain them.

Predictive models can also help companies identify top-performing candidates during the recruitment process, improving hiring decisions. Additionally, predictive analytics can forecast workforce needs, enabling organizations to plan for future talent requirements and align their HR strategies with business goals.

Benefits of Predictive Analytics

Organizations that leverage predictive analytics can gain several key benefits:

Data-Driven Decision Making

Predictive analytics enables organizations to make informed, data-driven decisions. By analyzing historical data and forecasting future outcomes, businesses can plan for the future with greater confidence.

Improved Operational Efficiency

Predictive models can identify inefficiencies and areas for improvement, allowing organizations to streamline operations and reduce costs. By anticipating demand fluctuations, equipment failures, and customer behavior, businesses can optimize their processes and resources.

Risk Mitigation

Predictive analytics helps organizations identify potential risks and take proactive steps to mitigate them. Whether it's forecasting financial losses, preventing equipment breakdowns, or detecting fraud, predictive models provide actionable insights that minimize risks.

Enhanced Customer Experience

Predictive analytics allows organizations to personalize customer interactions and provide tailored recommendations, improving customer satisfaction and loyalty. By predicting customer behavior, businesses can deliver relevant products and services, enhancing the overall customer experience.

Competitive Advantage
Organizations that harness the power of predictive analytics gain a competitive edge by anticipating market trends, optimizing operations, and making smarter decisions. Predictive insights enable businesses to stay ahead of competitors and capitalize on emerging opportunities.

Challenges of Predictive Analytics

Despite its many benefits, implementing predictive analytics comes with challenges:

Data Quality and Availability
The accuracy of predictive models depends on the quality of the data they are trained on. Incomplete or inaccurate data can lead to flawed predictions. Organizations must ensure they have access to high-quality data and implement proper data governance practices.

Complexity of Implementation
Building and maintaining predictive models requires specialized skills in data science, machine learning, and analytics. Organizations may need to invest in training or hire experts to implement and manage predictive analytics systems effectively.

Ethical and Privacy Concerns
Predictive analytics often involves analyzing sensitive data, raising concerns about data privacy and ethical use. Organizations must comply with data protection regulations and ensure that they use predictive analytics responsibly.

Predictive analytics is transforming how organizations make decisions by providing insights into future trends and behaviors. From optimizing operations and reducing risks to enhancing customer experiences and gaining a competitive edge, predictive analytics is a powerful tool that helps businesses navigate uncertainty with confidence. However, to fully realize the potential of predictive analytics, organizations must address challenges such as data quality, complexity, and ethical considerations. By embracing predictive analytics and continuously refining their models, organizations can unlock new opportunities for growth and success in an increasingly data-driven world.

Personalizing Customer Experience with AI

In an era where customer expectations are rapidly evolving, businesses are increasingly turning to artificial intelligence (AI) to deliver personalized experiences. Personalized customer experiences involve tailoring services, products, and interactions to the unique preferences and needs of each customer. AI's ability to process vast amounts of data, predict behavior, and provide real-time recommendations makes it an indispensable tool for organizations aiming to enhance customer satisfaction and loyalty.

This chapter explores how AI is reshaping customer experience (CX) personalization, the technologies that enable it, and its far-reaching impact across industries.

The Role of AI in Personalization

AI-powered personalization transforms the way businesses interact with customers by using machine learning algorithms, natural language processing (NLP), and predictive analytics. These technologies analyze vast amounts of customer data, such as purchase history, browsing behavior, preferences, and demographics, to provide highly customized and relevant experiences. The goal is to create a seamless and intuitive experience that anticipates customer needs, enhances engagement, and drives loyalty.

Unlike traditional approaches to customer personalization, AI adapts dynamically. It can learn from interactions in real time and adjust recommendations accordingly, allowing businesses to offer highly relevant content, products, and services based on individual preferences.

Key AI Technologies for Personalization

Several advanced technologies are driving AI-powered personalization:

Machine Learning (ML)
Machine learning algorithms are the backbone of AI-driven personalization. These algorithms analyze customer data to identify patterns and predict future behaviors. For example, based on a customer's browsing history, an ML model might recommend products they are likely to buy. Over time, as more data is collected, the system becomes better at making accurate predictions and refining personalization strategies.

Natural Language Processing (NLP)
NLP allows AI to understand and process human language. In the context of personalization, NLP can be used to analyze customer feedback, respond to

inquiries, and even create personalized marketing content. NLP-driven chatbots, for instance, can engage in meaningful conversations with customers, offering personalized assistance and product recommendations.

Predictive Analytics

Predictive analytics uses historical data to forecast future outcomes. In personalization, it predicts customer behavior, such as the likelihood of purchasing a product or churning. This enables businesses to offer timely promotions, product suggestions, or retention strategies. By analyzing trends and preferences, predictive analytics ensures that the customer journey is optimized at every touchpoint.

Recommendation Engines

Recommendation engines use collaborative filtering, content-based filtering, and hybrid methods to offer personalized product or content suggestions. Platforms like Netflix and Amazon are known for their sophisticated recommendation systems that tailor content to individual tastes based on previous behavior and the preferences of similar users.

Real-Time Data Processing

AI enables real-time personalization by processing data and generating insights as customers engage with a brand. Whether browsing a website, interacting with a chatbot, or making a purchase, AI can instantly update its recommendations and offers, ensuring a highly personalized experience with every interaction.

Applications of AI in Customer Personalization

AI-driven personalization spans across various industries, offering a range of applications that enhance customer experience:

E-Commerce and Retail
In e-commerce, AI personalizes the shopping experience by recommending products based on past purchases, browsing behavior, and demographic information. AI-powered systems can also predict customer needs and preferences, making relevant suggestions at different stages of the buying journey. For example, a customer who purchases running shoes might receive recommendations for sportswear, fitness trackers, or supplements.

Retailers also use AI for dynamic pricing, adjusting prices in real time based on factors such as customer behavior, demand, and competitor pricing. This ensures that customers receive personalized offers while maximizing business profits.

Entertainment and Media
Entertainment platforms like Netflix, Spotify, and YouTube use AI to personalize content recommendations. By analyzing viewing or listening habits, these platforms curate playlists, movies, or

shows that match individual tastes. AI also helps media companies personalize advertisements, ensuring that users see ads relevant to their preferences and behavior.

Healthcare

AI-powered personalization in healthcare can revolutionize patient care by providing personalized treatment plans and preventive care recommendations. By analyzing patient data, such as medical history, lifestyle, and genetic information, AI can help doctors create tailored treatment strategies that improve outcomes. Additionally, AI chatbots in healthcare can offer personalized wellness tips and reminders for medication or appointments, enhancing patient engagement.

Financial Services

In the financial sector, AI helps institutions offer personalized financial products and services. For instance, banks and insurance companies use AI to analyze customer financial behavior and recommend investment opportunities, credit products, or insurance policies tailored to individual needs. AI-driven robo-advisors provide personalized wealth management services, while AI chatbots assist customers with queries, offering real-time financial advice.

Travel and Hospitality

In the travel industry, AI-powered personalization

enhances the customer journey from start to finish. Travel agencies, airlines, and hotels use AI to recommend personalized travel packages, accommodation, and dining options based on a customer's past trips and preferences. AI also enables dynamic pricing in the travel sector, ensuring that customers receive competitive offers and promotions based on real-time demand and booking patterns.

Customer Service
AI-driven chatbots and virtual assistants play a key role in providing personalized customer service. These systems use NLP to engage customers in real-time conversations, answering inquiries, resolving issues, and providing tailored recommendations. AI-powered customer service solutions can predict customer needs based on past interactions and offer proactive support, such as reminding a customer of a renewal or suggesting an upgrade based on their usage patterns.

Benefits of AI-Driven Personalization

Increased Customer Satisfaction
By offering personalized experiences, businesses can significantly improve customer satisfaction. AI-driven personalization ensures that customers receive relevant products, services, and content, making them feel valued and understood. This fosters loyalty and strengthens the overall customer relationship.

Higher Conversion Rates
Personalized recommendations and tailored offers often lead to higher conversion rates. Customers are more likely to engage with content that resonates with their preferences, resulting in increased sales and customer retention. AI also allows businesses to present the right offer at the right time, boosting the chances of conversion.

Improved Customer Retention
AI helps businesses predict and prevent customer churn by analyzing behavior and identifying at-risk customers. By offering personalized incentives or addressing customer concerns before they lead to dissatisfaction, businesses can improve retention rates and foster long-term loyalty.

Enhanced Operational Efficiency

AI automates the personalization process, reducing the manual effort required to tailor experiences for individual customers. This allows businesses to scale personalization efforts without compromising quality. AI also provides real-time insights, enabling businesses to adapt their personalization strategies on the fly and respond quickly to changing customer preferences.

Data-Driven Insights

AI-powered personalization is built on data, and the insights generated from customer interactions provide valuable feedback. Businesses can use this information to refine their marketing strategies, improve product offerings, and optimize customer engagement. These data-driven insights ensure that personalization efforts remain relevant and effective over time.

Challenges of AI-Driven Personalization

Data Privacy and Security

The collection and analysis of customer data raise concerns about privacy and security. Businesses must ensure that they comply with data protection regulations, such as GDPR, and implement strong security measures to protect sensitive customer information. Transparency in data usage and obtaining customer consent are also critical for maintaining trust.

Data Quality and Availability

The effectiveness of AI-driven personalization depends on the quality of the data it processes. Incomplete or inaccurate data can lead to poor recommendations and negative customer experiences. Ensuring the availability of high-quality data is essential for delivering accurate and meaningful personalization.

Ethical Concerns

AI's ability to influence customer behavior through personalization raises ethical questions about manipulation and bias. Businesses must strike a balance between providing personalized experiences and respecting customer autonomy. It's important to ensure that AI algorithms are fair and unbiased, providing equal opportunities to all customers.

AI-driven personalization is reshaping how businesses engage with customers, offering tailored experiences that foster satisfaction, loyalty, and retention. By leveraging machine learning, predictive analytics, and real-time data processing, businesses can anticipate customer needs and provide relevant recommendations at every touchpoint. While challenges related to data privacy and ethics remain, the potential for AI to transform customer experience personalization is undeniable.

As AI technology continues to evolve, businesses that embrace AI-driven personalization will have a competitive advantage, delivering experiences that are not only personalized but also intelligent, responsive, and impactful.

How AI Can Drive Competitive Advantage

In the current digital age, the integration of artificial intelligence (AI) is no longer a futuristic vision—it is a vital tool for businesses aiming to stay competitive. AI provides organizations with a competitive advantage by streamlining operations, enhancing decision-making, personalizing customer experiences, and driving innovation. Companies that adopt AI are not only able to react to changes in the market faster but can also proactively shape the future of their industries.

This chapter delves into the various ways AI can be leveraged to create and sustain competitive advantage, from operational efficiency to strategic innovation.

Operational Efficiency and Cost Reduction

One of the primary benefits of AI is its ability to automate routine tasks, thereby driving operational efficiency and reducing costs. Through AI-driven automation, businesses can streamline processes, minimize human error, and increase output. For example, in industries like manufacturing, AI-powered robots and automated systems can handle tasks such as assembly, quality control, and logistics with speed and precision.

AI can also help optimize supply chains by predicting demand, monitoring inventory levels, and adjusting orders in real time. This leads to better resource management, reduces waste, and lowers operational costs. In customer service, AI chatbots can handle routine inquiries, freeing up human agents to focus on more complex issues, ultimately enhancing productivity and reducing labor expenses.

Data-Driven Decision Making

AI enhances decision-making by providing businesses with actionable insights derived from data. Through machine learning algorithms and predictive analytics, AI can process vast amounts of data at unprecedented speed, uncovering patterns and trends that humans might miss. This enables leaders to make informed decisions based on data rather than intuition or past experiences.

For example, in financial services, AI can analyze market trends and customer behavior to predict investment opportunities, assess risks, and recommend strategies for maximizing returns. Similarly, in retail, AI can analyze purchasing patterns to forecast demand and optimize pricing strategies, helping businesses stay ahead of competitors by reacting quickly to market shifts.

The ability to make data-driven decisions in real time provides businesses with a critical edge, allowing them to be more agile and responsive to both internal and external changes.

Enhanced Customer Experience

In an era where customer experience (CX) is a key differentiator, AI allows businesses to offer personalized and seamless interactions that drive customer satisfaction and loyalty. AI-powered recommendation engines, chatbots, and virtual assistants enable companies to anticipate customer needs and tailor services to individual preferences.

For instance, AI-driven algorithms analyze customer behavior—such as past purchases, browsing history, and social media activity—to deliver personalized product recommendations. This enhances the overall shopping experience, increases conversion rates, and boosts customer retention.

Furthermore, AI can power customer service platforms that provide real-time, 24/7 support. By quickly resolving inquiries and offering relevant solutions, AI improves customer engagement while reducing response times. AI can even predict potential issues before they arise, allowing businesses to proactively address customer concerns, which strengthens trust and builds long-term relationships.

Innovation and New Product Development

AI is a key enabler of innovation, helping businesses develop new products, services, and business models. By analyzing market data and consumer trends, AI can identify emerging opportunities that businesses can capitalize on. In product development, AI can simulate and optimize designs, leading to faster prototyping and testing cycles.

For example, in the pharmaceutical industry, AI is used to accelerate drug discovery by analyzing molecular structures and predicting the efficacy of potential treatments. This reduces the time and cost associated with bringing new drugs to market. Similarly, in the automotive industry, AI plays a crucial role in the development of autonomous vehicles by processing data from sensors to improve driving algorithms.

AI-driven innovation also enables businesses to create entirely new business models. For instance, the rise of AI-as-a-Service (AIaaS) platforms allows companies to integrate AI capabilities without having to invest heavily in infrastructure or expertise. By offering AI solutions on a subscription basis, businesses can create new revenue streams and differentiate themselves in competitive markets.

Predictive Maintenance and Risk Management

AI can significantly reduce downtime and minimize risks by predicting potential failures before they occur. In industries like manufacturing, energy, and transportation, AI-powered predictive maintenance solutions monitor equipment in real time and use machine learning algorithms to predict when a failure is likely to happen. This allows businesses to perform maintenance before a critical issue arises, reducing operational disruptions and saving costs.

In addition to maintenance, AI enhances risk management by identifying potential risks across various domains, including cybersecurity, compliance, and finance. For example, AI systems can analyze historical data and detect anomalies in real time, flagging potential cybersecurity threats or financial fraud before they cause significant damage.

By using AI to predict and mitigate risks, businesses can operate more efficiently, protect valuable assets, and maintain a competitive advantage in the marketplace.

AI-Powered Market Insights

AI provides businesses with deep insights into their market environment by analyzing data from a wide range of sources, including social media, customer reviews, financial reports, and industry publications. These insights can help companies better understand customer sentiment, track competitors' strategies, and identify emerging trends.

For example, sentiment analysis, powered by natural language processing (NLP), allows companies to monitor how customers perceive their brand or products in real time. This information helps businesses make adjustments to their marketing strategies or product offerings to better align with customer preferences. Similarly, AI can help businesses anticipate shifts in consumer demand or competitor moves, enabling them to act proactively and secure a first-mover advantage.

Moreover, AI can assist with competitor analysis by monitoring their marketing campaigns, product launches, and financial performance. This enables businesses to identify gaps in the market and exploit opportunities before their rivals do.

AI in Competitive Strategy

AI also plays a critical role in shaping competitive strategies. By leveraging AI tools for market analysis, customer segmentation, and operational insights, businesses can develop strategies that are more precise, data-driven, and forward-looking. This allows companies to position themselves more effectively in the market, anticipate shifts, and respond to competitors with agility.

AI-driven competitive strategies are particularly powerful in industries that are highly dynamic or data-intensive, such as technology, finance, and retail. For example, in the tech industry, AI can help companies optimize product development cycles and personalize user experiences, while in finance, AI can be used to develop more sophisticated trading algorithms and investment strategies.

By integrating AI into strategic planning, businesses can move beyond reactive decision-making to predictive and prescriptive strategies that put them ahead of their competition.

Challenges and Considerations

While AI offers immense potential for competitive advantage, there are also challenges and considerations that businesses must address to ensure successful implementation:

Data Privacy and Security

AI relies heavily on data, and with increasing concerns about privacy and security, businesses must ensure that they comply with regulations like GDPR and prioritize data protection. Companies must be transparent about how they collect and use customer data, while also investing in robust security measures to prevent data breaches.

Talent and Expertise

Implementing AI requires specialized talent in data science, machine learning, and AI development. However, there is a global shortage of AI experts, making it difficult for businesses to find the right talent to execute their AI strategies. Organizations may need to invest in training and development programs to build in-house expertise or partner with external providers to access AI capabilities.

Integration with Existing Systems

Many companies face challenges when integrating AI technologies into their existing infrastructure. AI systems must work seamlessly with legacy systems, and this can require significant investments in both time and resources. Businesses must also ensure that employees are trained to work alongside AI and leverage its capabilities effectively.

Ethical Considerations

The use of AI raises ethical concerns, particularly when it comes to bias, transparency, and decision-making. Businesses must ensure that their AI systems are fair and unbiased, particularly in areas such as hiring, lending, or law enforcement. Establishing ethical guidelines for AI implementation is critical for maintaining trust with customers and stakeholders.

AI is a game-changer in the business world, offering companies the ability to drive efficiency, enhance decision-making, and create innovative solutions that differentiate them from the competition. From automating routine tasks to providing deep insights into customer behavior and market trends, AI allows businesses to operate smarter, faster, and more strategically.

However, to fully realize the benefits of AI, businesses must carefully navigate challenges related to data privacy, talent acquisition, and ethical considerations. Companies that successfully integrate AI into their operations and strategy will not only gain a competitive advantage but will also be well-positioned to lead in the future of their industries.

As AI continues to evolve, the potential for competitive advantage will only grow, and the organizations that embrace this technology will shape the landscape of tomorrow's business world.

Integrating AI into Your Business Model

Artificial Intelligence (AI) is no longer a niche technology but a core component of modern business strategy. Integrating AI into your business model can revolutionize operations, enhance customer experiences, and drive innovation. However, the integration process involves careful planning, strategic alignment, and effective execution. This chapter provides a comprehensive guide on how to successfully integrate AI into your business model, including key considerations, practical steps, and common pitfalls to avoid.

Understanding the Strategic Value of AI

Before integrating AI into your business model, it's crucial to understand its strategic value. AI can:

Enhance Operational Efficiency: Automate routine tasks, streamline processes, and reduce operational costs.

Improve Decision-Making: Provide data-driven insights, predict trends, and support strategic planning.

Personalize Customer Experience: Tailor interactions and recommendations based on individual preferences and behavior.

Drive Innovation: Enable new products, services, and business models that can differentiate your brand.

Identifying where AI can add the most value to your business involves assessing your current operations, customer needs, and market opportunities.

Assessing Your Business Needs

Identify Key Areas for AI Integration:

Operational Efficiency: Look for repetitive tasks and processes that can be automated.

Customer Interaction: Identify touchpoints where personalization or real-time support can enhance the customer experience.

Data Utilization: Determine how AI can help leverage your data for better decision-making and predictive analytics.

Evaluate Your Current Technology Stack: Assess the compatibility of existing systems with AI technologies. Consider how AI solutions will integrate with your current infrastructure and whether upgrades or replacements are necessary.

Set Clear Objectives: Define what you aim to achieve with AI integration, whether it's reducing costs, increasing revenue, improving customer satisfaction, or all of the above. Establishing clear objectives will guide your implementation strategy and help measure success.

Choosing the Right AI Solutions

Select AI Technologies: Depending on your business needs, you might choose from a range of AI technologies, including:

Machine Learning (ML): For predictive analytics and pattern recognition.

Natural Language Processing (NLP): For chatbots, sentiment analysis, and language translation.

Computer Vision: For image recognition and visual data analysis.

Robotic Process Automation (RPA): For automating repetitive business processes.

Evaluate Vendors and Solutions: Research and select AI vendors that offer solutions aligned with your needs. Consider factors such as technology maturity, ease of integration, cost, and vendor support. Look for case studies and customer reviews to assess the effectiveness of their solutions.

Consider Custom AI Development: If off-the-shelf solutions do not meet your needs, consider developing custom AI models. This approach allows for tailored solutions but requires a higher investment in terms of time, resources, and expertise.

Developing an AI Integration Strategy

Build a Cross-Functional Team: Assemble a team with diverse expertise, including data scientists, IT professionals, business analysts, and domain experts. This team will oversee the integration process, ensuring alignment with business objectives and technical requirements.

Pilot Projects and Prototyping: Start with pilot projects to test AI solutions on a smaller scale before full-scale implementation. This approach allows you to validate the technology, measure its impact, and make necessary adjustments.

Data Preparation and Management: Ensure that your data is clean, accurate, and well-organized. AI models require high-quality data to deliver reliable results. Invest in data management systems and establish data governance practices to support AI initiatives.

Integration and Deployment: Develop a detailed integration plan that outlines how AI solutions will be incorporated into your existing systems and workflows. Ensure that the deployment process is seamless and that the AI systems are tested thoroughly before going live.

Change Management: Prepare your organization for the changes brought by AI integration. Communicate the benefits of AI to employees, provide training, and address any concerns. A well-managed change process helps in gaining buy-in from stakeholders and ensuring a smooth transition.

Measuring and Optimizing AI Performance

Define Key Performance Indicators (KPIs): Establish KPIs to measure the success of AI integration. These might include metrics related to efficiency gains, cost savings, customer satisfaction, and revenue growth. Regularly monitor these KPIs to assess the impact of AI on your business.

Continuous Improvement: AI systems should be continuously monitored and refined. Use feedback and performance data to improve the models and algorithms. AI technologies evolve rapidly, so staying updated with advancements and incorporating new features can help maintain a competitive edge.

Evaluate Return on Investment (ROI): Regularly assess the ROI of AI initiatives to ensure that they meet your strategic objectives. Compare the costs of AI implementation with the benefits achieved to determine whether the investment is justified.

Adapt and Scale: Based on performance and business needs, adapt your AI strategy and scale successful initiatives. Expand AI applications to other areas of your business where they can add value, and consider leveraging new AI technologies as they become available.

Common Pitfalls to Avoid

Lack of Clear Objectives: Without clear objectives, AI projects can become unfocused and fail to deliver tangible results. Ensure that you have well-defined goals and a strategic plan to guide your AI integration efforts.

Underestimating Data Requirements: AI solutions depend on high-quality data. Inadequate data or poor data management can lead to inaccurate results and hinder the effectiveness of AI systems.

Neglecting Change Management: Failing to address the organizational impact of AI integration can lead to resistance and operational disruptions. Implement a comprehensive change management strategy to support employees and facilitate a smooth transition.

Overlooking Ethical Considerations: AI systems can raise ethical issues related to bias, transparency, and privacy. Ensure that your AI solutions are designed and implemented with ethical considerations in mind to build trust and avoid potential legal and reputational risks.

Integrating AI into your business model offers significant opportunities for enhancing efficiency, decision-making, and innovation. By carefully assessing your needs, choosing the right technologies, and developing a strategic implementation plan, you can harness the power of AI to gain a competitive advantage.

Successful AI integration requires a clear vision, cross-functional collaboration, and ongoing optimization. By addressing common challenges and focusing on continuous improvement, your organization can effectively leverage AI to drive growth, enhance customer experiences, and stay ahead in a rapidly evolving business landscape.

Case Studies of Successful AI Implementations

AI technology has been transformative for numerous industries, offering innovative solutions and significant benefits. Examining real-world examples can provide valuable insights into how AI can be effectively integrated into business operations. This chapter presents a selection of case studies showcasing successful AI implementations across various sectors, highlighting the challenges faced, solutions developed, and outcomes achieved.

IBM Watson Health: Revolutionizing Healthcare Diagnostics

Company Background: IBM Watson Health is a division of IBM focused on harnessing AI and data analytics to improve healthcare delivery. The division aims to support medical professionals with advanced tools for diagnostics, treatment recommendations, and patient management.

Challenge: The healthcare industry faces challenges with the vast amounts of data generated by medical records, research, and clinical trials. Processing and analyzing this data manually is time-consuming and prone to errors, leading to delays in diagnosis and treatment.

Solution: IBM Watson Health deployed its AI platform, Watson for Oncology, to assist oncologists in diagnosing and treating cancer. Watson for Oncology uses natural language processing (NLP) and machine learning algorithms to analyze large volumes of medical literature, patient records, and clinical trial data.

Implementation:

Data Integration: Watson ingests and analyzes patient data, including medical histories and clinical notes.

Knowledge Base: The system is trained on a comprehensive knowledge base of medical literature and clinical guidelines.

Decision Support: Watson provides evidence-based treatment recommendations and identifies relevant clinical trials for personalized patient care.

Outcome:

Enhanced Accuracy: Watson for Oncology has improved diagnostic accuracy and treatment recommendations by analyzing data more thoroughly than traditional methods.

Efficiency Gains: The system significantly reduces the time required for oncologists to review and analyze medical literature, leading to faster decision-making.

Global Reach: Watson's AI solutions are being used in healthcare institutions worldwide, demonstrating its scalability and adaptability.

Netflix: Personalized Content Recommendations

Company Background: Netflix is a leading streaming service provider known for its vast library of films, TV shows, and original content. The company relies on AI to enhance user experience and drive engagement.

Challenge: With millions of users and a vast content library, Netflix needed an effective way to personalize recommendations to keep users engaged and satisfied. Traditional recommendation systems struggled to handle the scale and complexity of user preferences and viewing habits.

Solution: Netflix implemented a sophisticated recommendation engine powered by machine learning algorithms. The system analyzes user behavior, viewing history, and preferences to deliver personalized content suggestions.

Implementation:

Data Collection: Netflix collects data on user interactions, including viewing history, ratings, and search queries.

Machine Learning Algorithms: The recommendation engine uses collaborative filtering, content-based filtering, and deep learning techniques to analyze user preferences.

Real-Time Recommendations: The system provides real-time content recommendations, adapting to changes in user behavior and preferences.

Outcome:

Increased Engagement: Personalized recommendations have significantly increased user engagement and retention, leading to higher subscription rates.

Enhanced User Experience: The tailored content suggestions improve user satisfaction by helping viewers discover relevant and interesting content.

Competitive Advantage: Netflix's advanced recommendation system has become a key differentiator in the highly competitive streaming market.

Amazon: Optimizing Supply Chain with AI

Company Background: Amazon is a global e-commerce giant known for its extensive product offerings and efficient logistics network. The company utilizes AI to enhance its supply chain operations and improve customer experience.

Challenge: Managing a vast inventory and ensuring timely delivery to customers presents significant logistical challenges. Amazon needed to optimize its supply chain processes to handle high volumes of orders and minimize operational costs.

Solution: Amazon deployed AI and machine learning technologies to optimize inventory management, demand forecasting, and warehouse operations. Key AI applications include:

Demand Forecasting: Machine learning algorithms predict product demand based on historical sales data, seasonal trends, and external factors.

Inventory Optimization: AI analyzes inventory levels and adjusts stock based on demand forecasts, reducing excess inventory and stockouts.

Warehouse Automation: AI-powered robots and automated systems streamline warehouse operations, including picking, packing, and sorting.

Implementation:

Data Integration: Amazon integrates data from various sources, including sales records, customer behavior, and market trends.

Algorithm Training: Machine learning models are trained to predict demand and optimize inventory levels.

Automation: AI-driven robots and automated systems are deployed in fulfillment centers to enhance operational efficiency.

Outcome:

Improved Efficiency: AI has streamlined supply chain operations, reducing delivery times and operational costs.

Enhanced Forecasting: Accurate demand forecasting has minimized stockouts and excess inventory, leading to better inventory management.

Scalability: Amazon's AI-driven supply chain solutions have enabled the company to scale its operations globally while maintaining high levels of efficiency.

Tesla: Advancing Autonomous Driving

Company Background: Tesla is a leading electric vehicle manufacturer renowned for its innovations in autonomous driving technology. The company leverages AI to develop and enhance its self-driving capabilities.

Challenge: Developing a reliable and safe autonomous driving system requires processing vast amounts of data from vehicle sensors and cameras in real-time. Tesla needed an advanced AI system to enable its vehicles to navigate complex driving environments safely.

Solution: Tesla implemented an AI-powered Autopilot system that uses deep learning algorithms and computer vision to enable autonomous driving. The system processes data from cameras, radar, and ultrasonic sensors to understand and navigate the driving environment.

Implementation:

Data Collection: Tesla vehicles collect real-time data from sensors and cameras, including information on road conditions, traffic, and obstacles.

Deep Learning Models: The Autopilot system uses deep learning models to analyze and interpret sensor data, making driving decisions based on visual and environmental cues.

Continuous Improvement: Tesla continuously updates its Autopilot system with new data and algorithms to improve performance and safety.

Outcome:

Enhanced Safety: The AI-driven Autopilot system has improved vehicle safety by assisting with lane-keeping, adaptive cruise control, and automatic braking.

Autonomous Features: Tesla's advanced autonomous driving features have positioned the company as a leader in the electric vehicle market.

User Experience: The Autopilot system enhances the driving experience by reducing the burden on drivers and providing advanced driver assistance features.

Starbucks: Enhancing Customer Engagement with AI

Company Background: Starbucks is a global coffeehouse chain known for its commitment to customer satisfaction and innovation. The company uses AI to enhance customer engagement and streamline operations.

Challenge: Starbucks needed a way to personalize customer interactions and improve operational efficiency. With a large customer base and numerous locations, managing customer preferences and optimizing store operations presented significant challenges.

Solution: Starbucks implemented an AI-powered system to enhance customer engagement and optimize store operations. Key AI applications include:

Personalized Recommendations: The AI system analyzes customer purchase history and preferences to provide personalized product recommendations and offers.

Predictive Ordering: AI predicts customer demand and adjusts inventory levels accordingly, reducing waste and improving stock management.

Voice-Activated Ordering: The company introduced a voice-activated ordering system powered by natural language processing (NLP) to facilitate seamless customer interactions.

Implementation:

Customer Data Analysis: Starbucks collects and analyzes customer data to understand preferences and behavior.

Recommendation Engine: AI algorithms generate personalized recommendations and promotions based on individual customer profiles.

Operational Optimization: AI tools are used to predict demand, manage inventory, and optimize staffing levels.

Outcome:

Increased Customer Engagement: Personalized recommendations and offers have enhanced customer satisfaction and loyalty.

Operational Efficiency: Predictive ordering and inventory management have reduced waste and improved store operations.

Innovative Experience: The voice-activated ordering system has streamlined the ordering process, providing a modern and convenient customer experience.

These case studies illustrate the diverse applications of AI across various industries, from healthcare and e-commerce to automotive and food services. Successful AI implementations showcase how businesses can leverage AI to drive efficiency, enhance customer experiences, and achieve strategic objectives.

By learning from these examples, organizations can gain insights into the potential of AI, the challenges associated with its integration, and the benefits it can deliver. Whether optimizing supply chains, personalizing recommendations, or advancing technology, AI offers transformative opportunities for businesses to stay competitive and drive innovation.

Data Privacy and Security Issues in AI

Artificial Intelligence (AI) systems often rely on vast amounts of data to function effectively, raising significant concerns about data privacy and security. As AI technology becomes more integrated into various aspects of business and daily life, addressing these concerns is critical to maintaining trust and ensuring compliance with regulations. This chapter explores the key data privacy and security issues associated with AI, including the challenges faced, potential risks, and best practices for mitigating these issues.

Data Privacy Concerns

Data Collection and Consent: AI systems require extensive data collection to train algorithms and make accurate predictions. However, the collection of personal data raises privacy concerns, especially when consent is not adequately obtained. Users may not always be aware of what data is being collected, how it is used, or how long it is retained.

Challenge: Ensuring that data collection practices are transparent and that users provide informed consent.

Solution: Implement clear privacy policies and obtain explicit consent from users before collecting their data.

Provide users with options to control and manage their data preferences.

Data Usage and Purpose Limitation: Data collected for one purpose may be used for other purposes without the user's knowledge, leading to potential misuse or unauthorized access. This practice can violate privacy expectations and regulatory requirements.

Challenge: Ensuring that data is used only for the purposes for which it was collected.

Solution: Adopt a purpose-limitation principle, ensuring that data is used strictly for the specified purposes. Regularly review and update data usage policies to reflect changes in AI applications.

Data Anonymization and De-Identification: Anonymization and de-identification are techniques used to protect user privacy by removing or masking personal identifiers. However, these methods are not foolproof and can be vulnerable to re-identification through data aggregation and advanced analysis.

Challenge: Protecting privacy while maintaining the utility of data for AI purposes.

Solution: Use robust anonymization techniques and regularly assess the effectiveness of these methods.

Combine anonymization with other privacy-preserving techniques, such as differential privacy.

Data Security Challenges

Data Breaches and Unauthorized Access: AI systems often handle sensitive and valuable data, making them attractive targets for cybercriminals. Data breaches and unauthorized access can lead to the exposure of personal and confidential information.

Challenge: Preventing and responding to data breaches and unauthorized access.

Solution: Implement strong cybersecurity measures, including encryption, access controls, and regular security audits. Establish incident response protocols to quickly address and mitigate the impact of breaches.

Secure Data Storage and Transmission: Data used by AI systems must be securely stored and transmitted to prevent unauthorized access and tampering. Insecure storage and transmission practices can compromise data integrity and confidentiality.

Challenge: Ensuring secure storage and transmission of data.

Solution: Use encryption to protect data both at rest and in transit. Implement secure storage solutions and follow best practices for data handling and transmission.

Vulnerabilities in AI Models: AI models themselves can be vulnerable to attacks, such as adversarial attacks that manipulate model inputs to produce incorrect outputs. These vulnerabilities can undermine the security and reliability of AI systems.

Challenge: Protecting AI models from adversarial attacks and other security threats.

Solution: Employ techniques such as adversarial training and robust model validation to enhance model security. Regularly test and update models to address potential vulnerabllities.

Regulatory and Compliance Issues

Data Protection Regulations: Regulations such as the General Data Protection Regulation (GDPR) and the California Consumer Privacy Act (CCPA) impose strict requirements on data privacy and security. Compliance with these regulations is essential to avoid legal penalties and build trust with users.

Challenge: Ensuring compliance with data protection regulations.

Solution: Stay informed about relevant regulations and implement practices to meet their requirements. Conduct regular compliance audits and update policies and procedures as needed.

Cross-Border Data Transfers: Transferring data across borders can complicate compliance with data protection regulations, as different jurisdictions may have varying privacy and security requirements.

Challenge: Managing cross-border data transfers while ensuring compliance with international regulations.

Solution: Use data transfer mechanisms, such as Standard Contractual Clauses (SCCs) and Binding Corporate Rules (BCRs), to ensure compliance with cross-border data transfer requirements. Evaluate data transfer agreements and ensure they align with regulatory standards.

Best Practices for Data Privacy and Security

Implement Privacy by Design: Incorporate privacy considerations into the design and development of AI systems from the outset. This approach ensures that privacy and security are integral to the AI system's architecture and functionality.

Practice: Design AI systems with data protection features, such as encryption and access controls, embedded into their core functionalities.

Conduct Regular Privacy and Security Audits: Regularly audit AI systems and data handling practices to identify and address privacy and security vulnerabilities. Audits help ensure ongoing compliance with regulations and best practices.

Practice: Schedule periodic audits of AI systems, data storage, and security measures. Use audit findings to make necessary improvements and updates.

Educate and Train Employees: Provide training and awareness programs for employees on data privacy and security best practices. Ensure that all staff members understand their roles and responsibilities in protecting data.

Practice: Conduct regular training sessions on data privacy, security protocols, and regulatory requirements. Encourage a culture of data protection within the organization.

Establish Clear Data Governance Policies: Develop and implement data governance policies that define how data is collected, stored, used, and shared. Ensure that these policies align with privacy and security requirements.

Practice: Create comprehensive data governance policies and procedures, including data access controls, data retention policies, and incident response plans.

As AI technology continues to evolve, addressing data privacy and security issues is crucial to maintaining trust, ensuring compliance, and safeguarding sensitive information. By understanding the challenges and implementing best practices, organizations can effectively integrate AI into their operations while protecting data privacy and security.

A proactive approach to data privacy and security, combined with ongoing monitoring and adaptation, will help organizations navigate the complexities of AI and build a foundation for responsible and secure AI implementation.

Ethical Implications of AI

As Artificial Intelligence (AI) technologies advance and become increasingly integrated into various aspects of society, they bring about significant ethical considerations. These implications touch upon issues of fairness, transparency, accountability, and the impact on individuals and society at large. Understanding and addressing these ethical concerns is crucial for ensuring that AI technologies are developed and deployed in ways that align with societal values and promote the common good. This chapter explores the key ethical implications of AI, including the challenges and potential solutions.

Fairness and Bias

Algorithmic Bias: AI systems can inadvertently perpetuate or amplify biases present in the data they are trained on. Algorithmic bias occurs when AI models make decisions or predictions that disproportionately disadvantage certain groups, leading to unfair outcomes.

Challenge: Ensuring that AI systems do not reinforce existing biases or create new forms of discrimination.

Solution: Implement fairness audits and bias detection techniques during the development and testing of AI models. Use diverse and representative datasets to train algorithms and regularly evaluate model performance to identify and mitigate biases.

Discrimination and Inclusion: AI systems used in areas such as hiring, lending, and law enforcement can impact individuals' opportunities and rights. Discriminatory practices can lead to unequal treatment and exacerbate social inequalities.

Challenge: Preventing AI systems from discriminating against marginalized or underrepresented groups.

Solution: Adopt inclusive design practices and involve diverse stakeholders in the development process. Ensure transparency in AI decision-making and provide mechanisms for individuals to challenge and appeal decisions.

Transparency and Explainability

Black-Box Problem: Many AI models, especially those based on deep learning, operate as "black boxes," meaning their decision-making processes are not easily understandable by humans. This lack of transparency can hinder trust and accountability.

Challenge: Making AI systems' decision-making processes transparent and understandable to users.

Solution: Develop and adopt explainable AI techniques that provide insights into how models arrive at their decisions. Provide clear documentation and communication about AI systems' capabilities, limitations, and decision-making processes.

Accountability and Responsibility: Determining who is responsible for the actions and outcomes of AI systems is a complex issue. Accountability is crucial for addressing errors, biases, and unintended consequences.

Challenge: Establishing clear lines of accountability for AI systems and their impacts.

Solution: Define and enforce accountability frameworks that specify roles and responsibilities for AI development, deployment, and oversight. Implement governance structures that include oversight committees and ethical review boards.

Privacy and Data Protection

Data Privacy: AI systems often rely on large volumes of personal data, raising concerns about data privacy and the potential for misuse or unauthorized access. Ensuring that data is collected, stored, and used in compliance with privacy regulations is essential.

Challenge: Protecting individuals' privacy while utilizing data for AI purposes.

Solution: Implement robust data protection measures, such as encryption and anonymization, and ensure compliance with privacy regulations like GDPR and CCPA. Provide users with control over their data and transparency about its use.

Surveillance and Tracking: AI technologies can be used for surveillance and tracking, leading to concerns about the erosion of privacy and civil liberties. The use of AI for monitoring and surveillance requires careful consideration of ethical and legal implications.

Challenge: Balancing the benefits of surveillance with the need to protect individual privacy and freedoms.

Solution: Establish clear policies and regulations governing the use of AI for surveillance. Ensure that surveillance practices are justified, proportional, and subject to oversight and accountability.

Impact on Employment and the Workforce

Job Displacement: AI and automation can lead to job displacement as tasks previously performed by humans are taken over by machines. This shift has implications for workers and requires strategies to address the impact on employment.

Challenge: Managing the impact of AI on employment and ensuring a fair transition for displaced workers.

Solution: Develop and support retraining and reskilling programs to help workers transition to new roles. Promote policies that support job creation in emerging fields and address the socioeconomic effects of automation.

Changing Workforce Dynamics: AI can change the nature of work, leading to new job roles and changing skill requirements. Understanding and adapting to these changes is essential for maintaining a dynamic and adaptable workforce.

Challenge: Adapting to changes in job roles and skill requirements due to AI.

Solution: Encourage continuous learning and professional development to keep pace with technological advancements. Foster collaboration between educational institutions, employers, and policymakers to align skills training with future job needs.

Ethical Use of AI in Decision-Making

Autonomous Systems: AI systems that operate autonomously, such as self-driving cars and autonomous drones, raise ethical questions about decision-making in critical situations. Ensuring that these systems make ethical and responsible decisions is crucial.

Challenge: Ensuring that autonomous AI systems make decisions that align with ethical principles and societal values.

Solution: Develop ethical guidelines and decision-making frameworks for autonomous systems. Incorporate human oversight and accountability mechanisms to address ethical dilemmas and ensure responsible operation.

Military and Warfare Applications: The use of AI in military applications, including autonomous weapons and surveillance, raises ethical concerns about the potential for misuse and the impact on global security.

Challenge: Managing the ethical implications of AI in military and warfare contexts.

Solution: Establish international agreements and regulations governing the use of AI in military applications. Promote transparency and dialogue on the ethical implications of AI in defense and security.

Addressing Global and Societal Impacts

Equity and Access: AI technologies have the potential to benefit various aspects of society, but unequal access to these technologies can exacerbate existing inequalities. Ensuring equitable access to AI benefits is a key ethical consideration.

Challenge: Promoting equitable access to AI technologies and addressing disparities in their benefits.

Solution: Support initiatives that provide access to AI technologies and resources in underserved communities. Promote policies that ensure equitable distribution of AI benefits and address digital divides.

Long-Term Societal Impacts: The long-term societal impacts of AI, including changes in social structures, cultural norms, and power dynamics, require careful consideration and planning.

Challenge: Understanding and addressing the long-term societal impacts of AI technologies.

Solution: Engage in foresight and impact assessments to anticipate and address potential societal changes. Foster interdisciplinary research and dialogue on the ethical implications of AI for long-term planning and policy development.

The ethical implications of AI are multifaceted and require a thoughtful and proactive approach to address effectively. By understanding and addressing issues related to fairness, transparency, privacy, employment, and global impacts, organizations and policymakers can ensure that AI technologies are developed and used in ways that align with ethical principles and societal values.

Promoting ethical AI requires ongoing dialogue, collaboration, and commitment to responsible practices. By embedding ethical considerations into the design, development, and deployment of AI systems, we can harness the potential of AI to benefit society while minimizing risks and ensuring that technology serves the common good.

Preparing Your Workforce for AI Integration

As AI technologies reshape industries, organizations face the challenge of integrating these advanced systems while ensuring that their workforce is equipped to adapt. AI has the potential to enhance productivity, streamline operations, and drive innovation, but it can also disrupt existing job roles and create uncertainty for employees. Successfully preparing your workforce for AI integration is critical to fostering a seamless transition, empowering employees, and maintaining a competitive edge.

This chapter will outline the key steps organizations can take to prepare their workforce for AI integration, from identifying necessary skills to fostering a culture of continuous learning.

Identifying Skills and Roles Impacted by AI

Assessing Current Job Roles: The first step in preparing your workforce for AI integration is to assess which job roles are likely to be impacted by automation and AI technologies. Some roles may be enhanced by AI, while others may be displaced or require significant skill adjustments.

Solution: Conduct a comprehensive assessment of job roles within the organization to determine how AI will impact day-to-day tasks and responsibilities. Identify roles that will benefit from automation and areas where employees will need to adapt to new technologies.

Identifying Key AI Skills: AI integration will require a shift in the skill sets of employees, with a greater focus on technical skills such as data analysis, machine learning, and AI literacy. Additionally, "soft skills" such as problem-solving, creativity, and adaptability will become increasingly valuable as employees collaborate with AI tools.

Solution: Identify the technical and non-technical skills needed for AI adoption. Encourage employees to develop data literacy, critical thinking, and digital fluency to work effectively alongside AI systems.

Upskilling and Reskilling Employees

Providing Targeted Training Programs: To bridge the skills gap created by AI integration, organizations should invest in targeted upskilling and reskilling programs. These programs should focus on both the technical skills required to work with AI systems and the broader business implications of AI.

Solution: Develop tailored training programs that focus on AI technologies, data science, and programming, as well as industry-specific AI applications. Offer workshops, online courses, and certification programs to help employees acquire the necessary skills.

Fostering Lifelong Learning: AI integration is not a one-time event but an ongoing process. As AI technologies continue to evolve, employees must embrace a mindset of lifelong learning to stay ahead of technological advancements.

Solution: Encourage a culture of continuous learning by providing employees with access to learning resources, online platforms, and opportunities for professional development. Promote flexible learning environments where employees can experiment with new tools and technologies.

Collaborating with Educational Institutions: Organizations can partner with universities, coding bootcamps, and online education providers to offer specialized training and certification programs in AI, machine learning, and related fields.

Solution: Establish partnerships with educational institutions to co-create curricula focused on AI skills and emerging technologies. Offer employees opportunities to enroll in courses, pursue AI certifications, or participate in research collaborations.

Encouraging Cross-Functional Collaboration

Creating AI Centers of Excellence: Organizations can establish AI centers of excellence (CoE) to serve as hubs for AI innovation, experimentation, and collaboration. These centers can bring together cross-functional teams to work on AI projects and share best practices.

Solution: Set up internal AI CoEs to facilitate knowledge sharing and collaboration between departments. Engage teams from IT, operations, marketing, and HR to work together on AI-driven initiatives and ensure that all parts of the business benefit from AI integration.

Fostering Interdisciplinary Teams: AI integration often requires collaboration between technical and non-technical teams. Interdisciplinary teams, composed of data scientists, software engineers, business leaders, and subject matter experts, can ensure that AI technologies are effectively implemented and aligned with organizational goals.

Solution: Encourage collaboration across departments by forming interdisciplinary teams that combine technical expertise with industry-specific knowledge. This cross-functional approach ensures that AI applications are practical, relevant, and impactful.

Managing Workforce Transition and Redefining Roles

Supporting Role Transitions: As AI automates certain tasks, employees may need to transition to new roles within the organization. Managing these transitions effectively is critical to minimizing disruption and ensuring that employees feel supported throughout the process.

Solution: Provide clear communication about how AI will affect specific roles and offer guidance on potential career paths within the organization. Support employees in transitioning to new roles through mentorship, training, and career development programs.

Redefining Job Descriptions: AI integration will lead to changes in job descriptions and responsibilities. Employees will need to focus on higher-order tasks that require human creativity, strategic thinking, and emotional intelligence while leaving repetitive or data-intensive tasks to AI systems.

Solution: Redefine job descriptions to reflect the new roles and responsibilities created by AI integration. Emphasize the value of human-AI collaboration and highlight how AI will enhance, rather than replace, employees' contributions.

Addressing Workforce Anxiety: AI can create uncertainty and anxiety among employees who may fear job loss or feel overwhelmed by technological change. Addressing these concerns is essential to maintaining employee morale and engagement.

Solution: Communicate openly and transparently about the organization's AI strategy and the steps being taken to support employees through the transition. Provide reassurance by emphasizing opportunities for growth and skill development, and offer counseling or career coaching services as needed.

Building a Culture of Innovation and Adaptability

Promoting AI Literacy Across the Organization: AI literacy is not just for technical teams. To create a truly AI-ready workforce, all employees should have a basic understanding of AI, its capabilities, and its limitations. This understanding will empower employees to contribute to AI initiatives and make informed decisions about AI applications.

Solution: Offer company-wide AI literacy programs that provide employees with an introduction to AI concepts and use cases. Encourage employees at all levels to explore how AI can be applied to their roles and departments.

Fostering an Innovation Mindset: AI integration requires a shift in mindset, with a focus on embracing change, experimentation, and innovation. Employees who are open to new ideas and willing to experiment with AI tools will be better positioned to leverage the full potential of AI.

Solution: Cultivate an innovation-friendly environment by encouraging experimentation with AI technologies. Provide opportunities for employees to propose and test AI-driven projects and reward innovation and creativity.

Leadership and Change Management: Strong leadership is essential for guiding the workforce through the AI integration process. Leaders must not only champion AI initiatives but also create an environment of trust, openness, and support as employees adapt to change.

Solution: Equip leaders with change management skills to help them lead AI initiatives effectively. Encourage leaders to communicate the organization's vision for AI integration, provide clarity on the benefits, and offer ongoing support for employees throughout the transition.

Preparing your workforce for AI integration is a complex but critical task that requires a proactive and strategic approach. By identifying the roles and skills impacted by AI, investing in upskilling and reskilling, fostering cross-functional collaboration, managing workforce transitions, and building a culture of innovation, organizations can ensure that their employees are well-prepared to thrive in an AI-powered future.

Embracing AI as an opportunity for growth rather than a threat will allow businesses and their workforce to harness the potential of AI technologies while driving long-term success. With the right preparation, organizations can create a workforce that is not only capable of adapting to AI but also empowered to lead the way in the AI revolution.

Emerging AI Technologies on the Horizon

As artificial intelligence continues to evolve, a new wave of emerging AI technologies is set to transform industries and reshape the future of innovation. These groundbreaking advancements promise to push the boundaries of what AI can achieve, unlocking new possibilities for businesses and society. This chapter explores some of the most promising AI technologies on the horizon and their potential impact.

Quantum AI

The Power of Quantum Computing: Quantum computing has the potential to revolutionize AI by solving problems that are currently beyond the reach of classical computers. Quantum AI leverages the principles of quantum mechanics to perform computations at unprecedented speeds, enabling breakthroughs in optimization, data analysis, and machine learning.

Potential Impact: Quantum AI could enhance everything from drug discovery to cryptography, allowing AI systems to solve complex problems faster and more accurately. Businesses could optimize supply chains, financial models, and cybersecurity measures with greater precision.

Quantum Machine Learning (QML): Quantum machine learning combines quantum computing with traditional AI techniques to accelerate learning processes and improve model performance. QML algorithms could analyze massive datasets in a fraction of the time it takes today's systems, leading to more efficient AI models.

Applications: QML could revolutionize fields like healthcare, logistics, and finance by enabling faster data analysis, pattern recognition, and decision-making. For example, it could accelerate the discovery of new drugs or optimize complex global networks.

AI-Powered Generative Models

Generative AI Models (GANs and Transformers): Generative AI models, such as Generative Adversarial Networks (GANs) and large transformer models like GPT (Generative Pre-trained Transformer), are designed to create new data by learning from existing datasets. These models can generate realistic images, videos, text, and even music.

Potential Impact: GANs are already transforming industries like entertainment, marketing, and design by generating hyper-realistic visual content and deepfakes. Large language models, like GPT, are revolutionizing natural language processing, enabling chatbots, content creation, and language translation.

Creative Applications: Generative AI is pushing the boundaries of creativity, enabling AI to assist in designing products, composing music, writing scripts, and even creating digital art. AI's ability to generate novel ideas could help businesses innovate and differentiate their offerings.

Applications: Fashion brands can use generative models to create new designs, while filmmakers can rely on AI to generate special effects or even entire scenes. In marketing, AI-generated content can personalize messaging at scale.

Autonomous AI Systems

AI-Powered Robotics: AI-powered robotics is rapidly advancing, with robots becoming more autonomous, intelligent, and adaptable. These robots can perform tasks in environments that are too dangerous, repetitive, or precise for humans, from manufacturing and logistics to healthcare and agriculture.

Potential Impact: Autonomous robots have the potential to revolutionize industries by improving efficiency, safety, and precision. In logistics, AI-driven robots can optimize warehouse operations, while in healthcare, robotic assistants can assist in surgeries and patient care.

Self-Learning AI Agents: Self-learning AI agents represent the next frontier in autonomy. These agents can adapt to new environments and tasks without human intervention by continuously learning from their experiences.

Applications: In autonomous vehicles, self-learning AI could enhance navigation and decision-making capabilities, making cars safer and more efficient. In the workplace, self-learning AI agents could automate complex workflows, enabling organizations to streamline operations.

Neuromorphic Computing

Brain-Inspired AI Architectures: Neuromorphic computing seeks to mimic the architecture of the human brain by developing AI systems that operate using artificial neurons and synapses. This approach allows AI to process information in a way that is more similar to how the human brain works, enabling faster and more energy-efficient computing.

Potential Impact: Neuromorphic computing could revolutionize AI systems by making them more efficient in processing complex sensory data, such as vision and speech. It could also lead to AI systems that are better at real-time decision-making and contextual understanding.

Energy Efficiency: One of the biggest challenges in AI today is the energy consumption required for training and running large models. Neuromorphic computing promises to address this issue by creating more energy-efficient AI systems that require significantly less power.

Applications: Neuromorphic chips could be used in wearable devices, smart homes, and autonomous systems, enabling AI to be embedded in everyday objects. This could lead to smarter, more responsive IoT devices and applications with lower energy costs.

AI in Edge Computing

AI at the Edge: Edge computing involves processing data closer to the source, such as IoT devices, rather than relying on centralized cloud servers. AI at the edge enables real-time decision-making by analyzing data locally, reducing latency and bandwidth requirements.

Potential Impact: AI-powered edge devices can revolutionize industries like healthcare, manufacturing, and transportation by enabling real-time insights and decision-making without the need for constant connectivity to the cloud. This can enhance performance in critical applications, such as autonomous vehicles or remote medical monitoring.

AI in IoT (AIoT): AIoT is the convergence of AI and the Internet of Things, where smart devices use AI to analyze data and make decisions autonomously. This combination enhances the functionality and intelligence of connected devices, allowing them to respond to changing conditions in real-time.

Applications: AIoT can optimize energy consumption in smart homes, improve patient care with AI-driven wearable health devices, and enhance industrial automation by allowing machines to self-regulate based on real-time data.

AI for Human-AI Collaboration

AI-Augmented Decision-Making: AI's role in decision-making is evolving, with new technologies designed to augment human judgment rather than replace it. AI can provide data-driven insights and recommendations, helping humans make better decisions in complex, high-stakes environments.

Potential Impact: AI-augmented decision-making can be applied in industries like healthcare, finance, and legal services, where professionals rely on accurate data analysis to make critical decisions. AI tools can support clinicians in diagnosing diseases, assist lawyers in reviewing documents, and help financial analysts optimize investments.

Human-Centric AI Design: As AI systems become more sophisticated, there is a growing focus on designing AI technologies that prioritize human values, needs, and experiences. Human-centric AI design ensures that AI tools are intuitive, transparent, and aligned with ethical standards.

Applications: In healthcare, AI systems that are designed with the user in mind can assist doctors in providing more personalized care. In the workplace, AI tools that prioritize user experience can enhance employee productivity and satisfaction.

AI in Advanced Cybersecurity

AI-Driven Threat Detection: Cybersecurity is one of the most critical areas for AI advancement. AI can detect anomalies and potential threats by analyzing large amounts of data in real-time, offering faster and more accurate responses to security breaches.

Potential Impact: AI-powered cybersecurity systems can significantly enhance an organization's ability to prevent, detect, and respond to cyber threats. This is particularly important in sectors like finance, healthcare, and government, where sensitive data must be protected from increasingly sophisticated cyberattacks.

Automated Incident Response: AI can go beyond threat detection by automating the response process. AI systems can immediately contain and mitigate cyberattacks, reducing the damage caused and the time needed to resolve incidents.

Applications: AI-driven cybersecurity solutions can protect critical infrastructure, secure financial transactions, and safeguard personal data from breaches. They can also provide real-time monitoring of networks, systems, and devices to ensure continuous protection.

The future of AI is full of exciting possibilities, with emerging technologies that promise to revolutionize industries and enhance human capabilities. From quantum AI and neuromorphic computing to AI-powered robotics and edge computing, these innovations will shape the next decade of technological progress.

By staying ahead of these trends and embracing the opportunities they present, businesses can leverage AI to gain a competitive advantage, drive innovation, and prepare for the challenges and opportunities of tomorrow's AI-powered world.

Long-Term Impacts of AI on Business Growth

The rise of artificial intelligence (AI) is transforming industries, economies, and society at an unprecedented pace. While many businesses have already begun reaping the short-term benefits of AI in terms of efficiency and automation, the long-term impacts of AI on business growth extend far beyond these initial gains. AI has the potential to revolutionize entire business models, redefine competitive landscapes, and create new opportunities for innovation and revenue generation.

This chapter delves into the far-reaching effects of AI on business growth and how companies can position themselves to capitalize on AI's long-term potential.

AI-Driven Innovation and New Business Models

Fostering Continuous Innovation: One of the most significant long-term impacts of AI is its ability to drive continuous innovation. By automating routine tasks and freeing up human resources, AI allows businesses to focus on higher-value activities such as research, development, and creative problem-solving. AI systems can also identify emerging trends, patterns, and opportunities in real-time, helping companies stay ahead of the curve.

Long-Term Impact: Companies that integrate AI into their innovation processes will be better positioned to develop new products, services, and solutions that meet changing market demands. This ability to innovate rapidly will become a key differentiator in highly competitive industries.

AI-Enabled Business Models: AI is enabling the creation of entirely new business models, particularly in data-driven sectors. Subscription services, personalized products, and AI-as-a-service offerings are examples of how AI is reshaping traditional revenue streams. Businesses that can harness AI to offer tailored solutions or predictive services are likely to see long-term growth.

Applications: In retail, AI-powered recommendation engines can create hyper-personalized shopping experiences. In finance, AI algorithms can offer individualized investment advice. These new business models can lead to higher customer engagement, loyalty, and revenue.

Enhancing Customer Experience and Engagement

Personalization at Scale: As AI advances, businesses will be able to deliver highly personalized customer experiences at scale. By analyzing customer data, AI can predict preferences, behaviors, and needs, allowing businesses to offer customized products, services, and recommendations. Over the long term, this capability will transform how businesses interact with their customers, fostering stronger relationships and brand loyalty.

Long-Term Impact: Businesses that prioritize personalization will not only retain existing customers but also attract new ones. The ability to offer seamless, personalized experiences will become a competitive advantage, driving long-term growth.

AI-Powered Customer Support: AI technologies such as natural language processing (NLP) and chatbots are revolutionizing customer service by providing instant, accurate responses to customer inquiries. Over time, AI-driven customer support systems will become more sophisticated, offering human-like interactions and proactive problem-solving.

Applications: AI-driven customer service can handle routine inquiries, freeing human agents to focus on more complex issues. This improved efficiency can lead to higher customer satisfaction and lower operational costs, contributing to long-term business success.

Transforming Operations and Supply Chain Management

AI-Optimized Supply Chains: AI has the potential to revolutionize supply chain management by optimizing inventory levels, predicting demand, and identifying inefficiencies. AI systems can analyze vast amounts of data in real-time, enabling businesses to make faster, data-driven decisions about production, distribution, and logistics.

Long-Term Impact: Businesses that leverage AI to optimize their supply chains will see significant improvements in efficiency, cost reduction, and agility. Over the long term, AI-driven supply chains will enable companies to respond more effectively to market changes and disruptions, ensuring sustained growth.

Predictive Maintenance: In manufacturing and other asset-intensive industries, AI can be used to predict equipment failures and schedule maintenance proactively. Predictive maintenance, powered by machine learning algorithms, can reduce downtime, extend the life of assets, and lower maintenance costs.

Applications: AI-powered predictive maintenance is being used in industries such as automotive, aerospace, and energy to prevent costly breakdowns and ensure continuous operation. This long-term improvement in operational efficiency can lead to increased profitability and business growth.

Improving Decision-Making with AI

Data-Driven Insights: AI's ability to process and analyze large datasets in real-time allows businesses to make more informed and accurate decisions. As AI tools continue to improve, businesses will increasingly rely on predictive analytics and machine learning models to guide strategic decisions, from product development to market expansion.

Long-Term Impact: Businesses that embrace AI-driven decision-making will gain a significant advantage over competitors who rely solely on human intuition or traditional analytics. Over time, these data-driven insights will help companies optimize their operations, reduce risk, and identify new growth opportunities.

Real-Time Market Intelligence: AI can provide businesses with real-time market intelligence by analyzing competitor actions, customer feedback, and industry trends. This ability to monitor the market and respond to changes in real-time can give businesses a competitive edge in fast-moving industries.

Applications: In retail, AI can analyze market conditions to recommend pricing strategies. In finance, AI tools can detect market trends and suggest investment opportunities. The long-term impact of these capabilities will be greater agility, responsiveness, and sustained business growth.

Creating a Competitive Advantage with AI

AI as a Competitive Differentiator: In the long term, companies that successfully integrate AI into their core operations will have a competitive edge over those that do not. AI can enhance everything from customer experience and supply chain management to product development and marketing strategies, allowing businesses to outperform competitors.

Long-Term Impact: Businesses that use AI to create unique value propositions will establish themselves as leaders in their industries. As AI technology becomes more widespread, the ability to leverage AI for competitive advantage will be essential for long-term business growth.

Building Barriers to Entry: AI can also help businesses build barriers to entry by creating proprietary AI systems, data sets, and technologies that are difficult for competitors to replicate. This can protect a company's market position and ensure long-term profitability.

Applications: Proprietary AI algorithms in industries such as finance, healthcare, and e-commerce can create lasting competitive advantages. Companies that invest in developing AI-driven intellectual property will secure their market leadership for the future.

Evolving Workforce and Organizational Structure

AI-Enhanced Workforce: In the long term, AI will transform the workforce by augmenting human capabilities and automating routine tasks. AI systems can take over repetitive, data-intensive tasks, allowing employees to focus on more strategic and creative work. This shift will require companies to rethink their organizational structures and develop new roles that blend human expertise with AI capabilities.

Long-Term Impact: Companies that invest in AI training and upskilling will be better equipped to adapt to the changing workforce landscape. By combining human creativity with AI efficiency, businesses can unlock new levels of productivity and innovation, driving long-term growth.

Redefining Leadership Roles: As AI systems become more integral to business operations, leadership roles will evolve to include AI oversight and strategy. Executives will need to understand AI's potential, its limitations, and its ethical implications to guide their organizations through AI-driven transformations.

Applications: Future leaders will need to balance AI-driven insights with human judgment to make strategic decisions. Over time, organizations that foster a culture of AI literacy and innovation will be more agile and better positioned for sustained growth.

Ethical Considerations and Long-Term Trust

Navigating AI Ethics: As AI becomes more embedded in business operations, ethical considerations will become increasingly important. Issues such as bias in AI algorithms, data privacy, and the impact of automation on employment must be addressed to maintain public trust and avoid regulatory pitfalls.

Long-Term Impact: Companies that prioritize ethical AI practices will build stronger relationships with customers, employees, and stakeholders. This focus on ethical AI will be a key factor in ensuring long-term business sustainability and growth.

Building Consumer Trust: In the long term, businesses that use AI transparently and responsibly will gain consumer trust. As customers become more aware of AI's role in decision-making, companies that demonstrate ethical AI usage and data protection will differentiate themselves in the market.

Applications: Transparency in AI-driven decisions, such as personalized recommendations or pricing, will be crucial for building customer trust. Companies that maintain ethical AI practices will foster long-term loyalty and business growth.

AI's long-term impacts on business growth are profound and far-reaching. From driving innovation and optimizing operations to enhancing customer experiences and improving decision-making, AI is reshaping the way businesses operate and compete. Companies that embrace AI's potential and prepare for its long-term implications will be well-positioned to thrive in the rapidly evolving digital economy.

To capitalize on these opportunities, businesses must invest in AI technologies, upskill their workforce, and adopt ethical AI practices. By doing so, they can secure a competitive advantage, foster sustainable growth, and unlock new opportunities in the AI-powered future.

Recap of AI's Potential

Artificial Intelligence (AI) is poised to redefine how businesses operate, compete, and grow. Its potential spans across multiple facets of modern industry, driving innovation, efficiency, and long-term transformation. As AI technologies advance, businesses that effectively integrate AI into their operations stand to benefit from increased agility, customer engagement, and new revenue streams. Here's a recap of AI's immense potential:

Continuous Innovation

AI enables businesses to innovate faster by automating routine tasks and identifying emerging trends in real-time. Companies can focus on creating new products, services, and solutions, staying ahead of competitors and addressing evolving market demands.

Personalized Customer Experiences

AI excels in delivering highly personalized interactions at scale, offering customized recommendations, products, and services. Personalization fosters deeper customer loyalty and drives higher engagement, positioning businesses as market leaders.

Operational Efficiency and Optimization

AI enhances supply chain management, predictive maintenance, and decision-making. By optimizing operations through real-time data analysis and machine learning, businesses can reduce costs, increase efficiency, and improve responsiveness to market changes.

Data-Driven Decision-Making

AI provides businesses with real-time insights and predictive analytics, allowing them to make informed, accurate decisions. This leads to better strategies, reduced risk, and the identification of new growth opportunities.

Workforce Augmentation and Evolution

AI allows employees to focus on strategic, creative work by automating repetitive tasks. Businesses that invest in AI training and organizational restructuring will create a more productive, innovative workforce, leading to long-term growth.

Ethical AI and Building Trust

As AI becomes central to operations, ethical considerations such as bias, transparency, and data privacy are crucial. Companies that prioritize ethical AI practices will build consumer trust, leading to lasting relationships and a stronger market position.

In conclusion, AI's potential is transformative, from fostering continuous innovation to enabling better decision-making and enhancing operational efficiency. Businesses that recognize AI's long-term capabilities and responsibly adopt these technologies will unlock unprecedented growth opportunities and secure a competitive edge in the digital age.

Steps to Start Your AI Journey

Embarking on the AI journey is crucial for businesses that want to stay competitive in an increasingly digital world. Implementing AI requires careful planning, a clear strategy, and the right resources. Here are key steps to help you get started on integrating AI into your business:

Identify Business Objectives

Before diving into AI, it's essential to define clear business objectives. What do you want to achieve with AI? This could include improving operational efficiency, enhancing customer experiences, developing new products, or gaining competitive insights. Establishing specific goals will guide your AI strategy and ensure that your efforts align with broader business objectives.

Start by identifying areas in your business where automation, data analysis, or decision-making processes could be improved with AI.

Assess AI Readiness

Evaluate your organization's current technology infrastructure, data quality, and team capabilities. AI thrives on data, so having the right tools and quality data is essential. Additionally, your workforce should be familiar with AI concepts and open to adopting new technologies.

Conduct a readiness assessment to determine if your company has the data, technology, and skills necessary to start implementing AI. If there are gaps, invest in building the required infrastructure.

Build a Strong Data Foundation

Data is the fuel that powers AI. Collect, organize, and clean your data to ensure it's accurate, accessible, and well-structured. Having a solid data foundation is critical for effective AI algorithms, predictive models, and machine learning processes.

Consider implementing data governance practices and tools to ensure that your data is consistent, reliable, and free of biases.

Start Small with Pilot Projects

Rather than overhauling your entire business with AI from the start, begin with a pilot project that addresses a specific problem or process. Choose a use case that aligns with your business objectives and offers the potential for quick wins. This will allow you to test AI's impact on a small scale and learn from the experience.

Example: Automating customer support through AI-powered chatbots or enhancing demand forecasting with machine learning.

Choose the Right AI Tools and Technologies

There are a variety of AI tools and platforms available, each designed for different purposes—such as natural language processing, machine learning, or data analytics. Select AI tools that align with your business needs, budget, and technical capabilities. Many cloud-based AI solutions offer flexibility and scalability, making them ideal for businesses at the early stages of AI implementation.

Evaluate vendors carefully and ensure the tools integrate well with your existing systems.

Build a Skilled AI Team

To succeed with AI, you need a team with a mix of skills, including data science, AI development, and business expertise. If you don't have the talent in-house, consider partnering with AI consultants, hiring AI specialists, or upskilling your current employees.

Encourage a culture of continuous learning where team members stay updated on the latest AI developments and trends.

Ensure Ethical AI Practices

As you deploy AI solutions, prioritize ethics and data privacy. Be transparent about how AI is used in your business processes, avoid biases in AI algorithms, and comply with data protection regulations. Building trust with customers and stakeholders will be key to long-term AI success.

Establish a framework for ethical AI that includes regular audits, data privacy policies, and a clear approach to mitigating potential biases.

Measure Success and Optimize

Once your pilot projects are live, measure the outcomes against the goals you initially set. Analyze how AI has impacted efficiency, customer experience, or revenue growth. Use these insights to fine-tune your AI models, expand AI applications to other areas of your business, and improve overall performance.

Use metrics such as cost savings, increased efficiency, customer satisfaction, or time-to-market to gauge the effectiveness of your AI initiatives.

Scale AI Across the Organization

After successfully implementing pilot projects, you can begin scaling AI across different departments and functions within your business. Whether it's automating back-office processes, leveraging AI in marketing, or enhancing decision-making, expanding AI applications will drive significant long-term growth.

As you scale AI, ensure that it integrates seamlessly with existing systems and aligns with your long-term business strategy.

Stay Agile and Innovate Continuously

AI technology evolves rapidly, so it's essential to stay agile and adapt to new advancements. Continuously evaluate emerging AI tools, technologies, and techniques to ensure your business remains at the forefront of AI innovation. Encourage a culture of experimentation and iterative improvement, so your AI journey keeps pace with technological changes and market demands.

Invest in ongoing training, research, and partnerships with AI experts to stay ahead in the rapidly evolving AI landscape.

Starting your AI journey is a strategic move that requires careful planning, investment in data and talent, and a commitment to ongoing innovation. By following these steps, your business can unlock AI's full potential and position itself for long-term success in the digital economy. Whether you're just beginning or scaling AI across your organization, a thoughtful, step-by-step approach will help ensure a successful AI transformation.

Recommended Articles and Books on AI

Recommended Articles:

"The Age of AI and Our Human Future"

This article explores the profound societal changes AI will bring, from global politics to human decision-making. It offers deep insights into how AI might reshape human cognition and interaction in the digital age.

"Artificial Intelligence and the Future of Work"

A discussion on how AI is revolutionizing the workforce, this piece examines the challenges and opportunities AI presents, particularly around job automation, skill development, and the evolving relationship between humans and machines.

AI for Business: Key Trends and Future Predictions"

This article covers the latest AI trends in business, showcasing how industries are adopting AI for enhanced productivity, customer experience, and competitive advantage. It also highlights real-world applications of AI in various sectors.

"Building Ethical AI"

This article emphasizes the critical importance of developing AI systems that are transparent, fair, and unbiased. It provides strategies for implementing ethical AI frameworks that ensure trustworthiness in AI decision-making processes.

"AI and the Transformation of Cybersecurity"

An in-depth exploration of how AI is transforming the cybersecurity industry, focusing on the application of AI for threat detection, predictive analytics, and automated responses to security breaches.

Recommended Books:

"Superintelligence: Paths, Dangers, Strategies" by Nick Bostrom

This book delves into the risks and rewards of AI surpassing human intelligence. It addresses the ethical considerations and strategic decisions humanity must make as AI advances toward superintelligence.

"Human + Machine: Reimagining Work in the Age of AI" by Paul Daugherty and H. James Wilson

This work explores how AI will reshape the future of work, emphasizing collaboration between humans and machines. It provides practical insights on how businesses can leverage AI to drive innovation and increase productivity.

"The Fourth Industrial Revolution" by Klaus Schwab

Schwab outlines the role of AI and other emerging technologies in the fourth industrial revolution, discussing their impact on economies, industries, and societies. He also examines the ethical and governance challenges posed by these technological advancements.

"AI Superpowers: China, Silicon Valley, and the New World Order" by Kai-Fu Lee

This book contrasts the AI developments in the U.S. and China, two of the world's leading AI hubs. Lee offers unique perspectives on how AI is shaping the global economy and the future of innovation.

"Life 3.0: Being Human in the Age of Artificial Intelligence" by Max Tegmark

Tegmark's book explores the future of AI, focusing on how it will affect life, society, and our understanding of what it means to be human. He examines both the opportunities and dangers of AI's rapid development, making it an essential read for those interested in the ethical and philosophical implications of AI.

AI Tools and Platforms to Explore

If you're looking to get hands-on with AI, there are a number of powerful tools and platforms that can help businesses and individuals start building AI-driven solutions. These platforms offer a range of capabilities from machine learning (ML) to natural language processing (NLP) and computer vision, often without requiring deep technical expertise.

TensorFlow

Type: Open-Source Machine Learning Library

Developed By: Google

Overview: TensorFlow is one of the most popular libraries for building machine learning models, offering tools for both beginners and experts. It supports deep learning, neural networks, and other complex AI models. TensorFlow also has pre-trained models and an easy-to-use interface for quick prototyping.

Best For: Data scientists, researchers, and AI developers.

IBM Watson

Type: AI and NLP Platform

Developed By: IBM

Overview: IBM Watson is a suite of enterprise-grade AI tools designed to handle complex NLP tasks like speech-to-text, sentiment analysis, and chatbot creation. It's particularly useful for businesses looking to leverage AI for customer service, data analysis, and decision-making.

Best For: Enterprises looking for scalable AI solutions for customer service, finance, and healthcare.

Microsoft Azure AI

Type: Cloud-Based AI Services

Developed By: Microsoft

Overview: Azure AI offers a wide array of AI services, from machine learning and NLP to computer vision and anomaly detection. With its pre-built APIs and easy integration with other Microsoft services, Azure AI is a great tool for businesses looking to deploy AI solutions quickly and efficiently.

Best For: Organizations seeking cloud-based AI solutions with easy integration into existing Microsoft products.

Google Cloud AI

Type: Cloud-Based AI Services

Developed By: Google

Overview: Google Cloud AI provides a suite of AI tools that include machine learning, NLP, and computer vision capabilities. It also offers pre-trained models and APIs for businesses to integrate AI into their applications. Google Cloud's AutoML is particularly useful for automating machine learning tasks for non-experts.

Best For: Companies looking for scalable AI tools with access to Google's infrastructure and vast data sets.

H2O.ai

Type: Open-Source Machine Learning Platform

Overview: H2O.ai is an open-source machine learning platform that allows businesses to build predictive models using AI and big data. It is widely known for its automated machine learning (AutoML) capabilities, which allow users to automate the model-building process.

Best For: Data-driven companies looking to automate machine learning processes and create powerful predictive models without extensive coding knowledge.

Amazon Web Services (AWS) AI

Type: Cloud-Based AI Services

Developed By: Amazon

Overview: AWS offers a comprehensive suite of AI tools, including Amazon SageMaker for building and training machine learning models, Amazon Polly for text-to-speech, and Amazon Rekognition for image and video analysis. These tools allow businesses to incorporate AI into their applications and workflows with ease.

Best For: Enterprises that rely on cloud services and need AI solutions that can easily integrate with AWS infrastructure.

OpenAI API

Type: AI and NLP Platform

Developed By: OpenAI

Overview: OpenAI provides cutting-edge NLP models like GPT (Generative Pre-trained Transformer), which can be used for a variety of text-based applications, including content generation, summarization, and chatbot development. The API allows developers to access powerful AI models without building them from scratch.

Best For: Developers looking to build applications using state-of-the-art NLP models and generative AI capabilities.

DataRobot

Type: Automated Machine Learning (AutoML) Platform

Overview: DataRobot simplifies the process of building and deploying machine learning models. With its AutoML features, it allows businesses to automate data preparation, model selection, and tuning. It's an excellent tool for those who want to leverage AI without needing extensive machine learning expertise.

Best For: Companies that want to implement machine learning quickly and efficiently across business functions.

PyTorch

Type: Open-Source Machine Learning Library

Developed By: Facebook AI Research

Overview: PyTorch is another leading machine learning framework, favored for its simplicity and flexibility, particularly for research and experimentation. It's widely used for deep learning applications and is known for dynamic computation graphs, which make it easier to debug and iterate.

Best For: Researchers, AI developers, and companies focusing on deep learning and neural networks.

BigML

Type: Machine Learning Platform

Overview: BigML offers user-friendly, cloud-based machine learning services for businesses that want to build predictive models. It offers features such as classification, regression, clustering, anomaly detection, and association discovery, all with an intuitive interface.

Best For: Small and medium-sized businesses looking for easy-to-use machine learning tools without requiring extensive AI expertise.

MonkeyLearn

Type: AI and NLP Platform

Overview: MonkeyLearn is a no-code platform that allows businesses to create custom machine learning models for text analysis. From sentiment analysis to keyword extraction, MonkeyLearn is great for companies looking to quickly implement AI-based text processing without technical complexity.

Best For: Marketing teams and businesses that need NLP solutions for customer feedback, surveys, and social media monitoring.

Whether you're just starting out or looking to scale your AI capabilities, these platforms offer a range of options to fit your business's needs. From cloud-based services like AWS, Azure, and Google Cloud to open-source libraries like TensorFlow and PyTorch, you can explore tools that align with your technical proficiency and business goals.

AI Tools and Platforms to Explore

As businesses and developers continue to integrate AI into various operations, it's crucial to know which tools and platforms can best help you build AI-driven solutions. Below is a comprehensive guide to the most powerful AI platforms and tools available, whether you're looking for machine learning, natural language processing, or computer vision capabilities.

TensorFlow

Developed By: Google

Description: An open-source platform widely used for building machine learning models. TensorFlow provides extensive tools for both beginners and experts, offering support for deep learning, neural networks, and more.

Use Case: Great for developing complex AI models in fields like computer vision, NLP, and autonomous systems.

IBM Watson

Developed By: IBM

Description: A comprehensive AI platform that excels in NLP, speech recognition, and AI-driven business solutions. Watson offers pre-built applications and customizable models for industries like healthcare, finance, and customer service.

Use Case: Ideal for enterprises needing AI solutions in customer service automation, data analytics, and business insights.

Microsoft Azure AI

Developed By: Microsoft

Description: Azure AI is a cloud-based platform offering various AI services, including computer vision, NLP, and machine learning. Its integration with Microsoft's ecosystem makes it a go-to for businesses already using Azure.

Use Case: Perfect for organizations using Microsoft products and looking for seamless AI integration.

Google Cloud AI

Developed By: Google

Description: Google Cloud AI provides a variety of services from AutoML to APIs for vision, speech, translation, and more. Google Cloud's AutoML allows non-experts to build custom machine learning models easily.

Use Case: Businesses seeking to automate tasks with machine learning models and leverage Google's extensive cloud infrastructure.

Amazon Web Services (AWS) AI

Developed By: Amazon

Description: AWS offers an extensive suite of AI tools, including Amazon SageMaker for building, training, and deploying ML models. Other services like Polly for text-to-speech and Rekognition for image recognition make AWS a comprehensive solution for AI development.

Use Case: Suitable for companies already utilizing AWS who want to incorporate AI for predictive analytics, computer vision, or customer experience improvements.

OpenAI GPT

Developed By: OpenAI

Description: GPT (Generative Pre-trained Transformer) models are highly versatile, excelling in natural language processing tasks like text generation, summarization, translation, and chatbots.

Use Case: Ideal for developers seeking cutting-edge NLP models for content creation, customer interaction automation, and more.

H2O.ai

Description: An open-source platform for building and deploying machine learning models, particularly known for its automated machine learning (AutoML) capabilities, which reduce the need for manual coding.

Use Case: Excellent for data scientists and businesses looking to build AI solutions quickly without deep expertise in AI.

DataRobot

Description: An enterprise-grade platform for automating the building, deployment, and monitoring of machine learning models. Its AutoML capabilities allow users to streamline the AI process from data input to actionable insights.

Use Case: Designed for businesses that need automated, scalable machine learning models for finance, marketing, or operations.

PyTorch

Developed By: Facebook AI Research

Description: A flexible, open-source machine learning library widely used for research and development in AI. Known for its dynamic computation graphs and ease of debugging, PyTorch is often preferred in academia and for deep learning projects.

Use Case: Best for developers and researchers working on cutting-edge deep learning models and experimental AI systems.

BigML

Description: A cloud-based platform offering a variety of machine learning services such as classification, regression, clustering, and anomaly detection. It provides a simple, user-friendly interface with automation features for building models.

Use Case: Suitable for small to medium-sized businesses that need an intuitive AI platform for predictive analytics and decision-making.

MonkeyLearn

Description: A no-code AI tool for building machine learning models focused on text analysis. MonkeyLearn specializes in sentiment analysis, keyword extraction, and topic modeling, making it an excellent choice for businesses processing large volumes of text data.

Use Case: Ideal for marketing teams and businesses looking to implement NLP solutions for customer feedback analysis, social media monitoring, and more.

These AI tools and platforms provide a wide range of solutions tailored to different business needs, technical expertise, and AI ambitions. Whether you're looking to enhance customer interactions, automate processes, or develop complex models, there's a platform to suit your needs, from highly accessible solutions like AutoML and MonkeyLearn to advanced frameworks like TensorFlow and PyTorch.

As we stand on the cusp of 2024, the integration of Artificial Intelligence into the fabric of our business landscapes promises to be nothing short of revolutionary. The insights shared throughout this book reflect not just the current state of AI but also the boundless potential it holds for reshaping industries and driving innovation.

The journey through AI's transformative impact on business operations, strategy, and the broader marketplace underscores a pivotal truth: embracing AI is not merely an option but a necessity for forward-thinking enterprises. As technology continues to evolve at an unprecedented pace, the key to thriving in this new era lies in adaptability and foresight.

We have explored the promising advancements in machine learning, the nuances of AI-driven automation, and the profound implications for customer personalization. Yet, beyond these technological marvels, the essence of AI's impact will be determined by how we navigate its challenges, from ethical considerations to workforce readiness. It is imperative for businesses to not only harness AI's capabilities but also address the broader implications it brings.

Looking ahead, the future of AI is not just about the technology itself but how we choose to leverage it in alignment with our values and goals. It is a call to action for leaders, innovators, and visionaries to shape a future where AI enhances human potential and drives meaningful progress.

As you close this book and reflect on the possibilities AI presents, remember that the journey of transformation is ongoing. The insights and strategies discussed here are just the beginning of what promises to be a thrilling era of discovery and growth. May you be inspired to lead with vision, embrace the opportunities ahead, and shape a future where AI elevates your business to new heights.

Thank you for embarking on this journey with us. The future is here, and it is powered by AI.